Essays in Social Justice

By J. A. Jones

Preface

This book is a compilation of my original research articles on various topics in criminal and social justice. Investigating the issues discussed herein laid the groundwork for my scholarly development and conjured within me a sense of civic duty. During the years that these essays span, not a single aspect of my political or ideological identity survived unaltered without at least being heavily scrutinized. Therefore, the thought of them collecting dust after being read only by myself and a handful of professors seemed tragic. I published them with the hope that they may be happened upon by curious passers-by and contribute, if only in some small way, to their intellectual maturation.

I do not claim to have all, or even a fair amount, of the answers to those questions which trouble every citizen entranced by the seemingly ever-more dismal evening news and political debates of perpetually degenerating productivity. All I can offer is my own humble perspective gained from the meticulous research conducted while I could have been otherwise engaged in non-productive activity and distraction. I caution, and simultaneously implore, the reader to absorb each point with skepticism. Do not take even a single assertion as undeniable fact. For, as the saying goes, there are three sides to every story; my side, your side, and the truth. Make up your own mind and, by all means, prove me wrong.

Acknowledgments

I very well could have ended up as a disgruntled veteran working my fingers to the bone in someone else's dream. I am therefore indebted to those select few who saw unutilized potential and motivated me to pursue a college education and commit my thoughts to writing. Four in particular stand out in my mind as deserving of more than I can repay. First, thanks to my father for explaining to a rebellious young man with no plans for an adult life that "If you're going to have a weak mind, you'd better have a strong back." Of course, I must also acknowledge that these words may never have met paper without my mother's unwavering confidence in her eldest son. And the fact that this book was actually published is due in large part to my unofficial manuscript reviewer and personal support system, Coeli, who walked onto the stage of my life with impeccable timing and encouraged me to put in the arduous, but necessary, work. Lastly, I would be remiss if I did not give proper credit to my canine companion, Hemi, for always reminding me that it is equally as important to set aside playtime. Otherwise, what is the point of it all?

Contents

Contents Cont'd

Part One:
American Justice & Recidivism Reduction

I

Wrongful Conviction in the American Judicial Process: History, Scope, and Analysis

Most Americans harbor the presumption that their criminal justice system is fair and blind. Therein, an assumption is made that no person shall ever be convicted for a crime that he or she did not commit (Huff, 2002; Marquis, 2005). The idea that a free citizen could be unjustly sentenced to prison or executed by the State is diametrically opposed to the concept of judicious treatment expected in the United States. Indeed, audiences sympathize with characters such as John Coffey (Michael Clarke Duncan) of "The Green Mile" and Andy Dufresne (Tim Robbins) of "The Shawshank Redemption" because the notion of wrongful incarceration is utterly terrifying, though ostensibly quarantined to the realm of fiction (Darabont, 1994; 1999).

Indeed, every person living in the United States, citizen or not, is afforded the constitutional rights of due process and a trial by a jury of their peers, wherein the State must prove beyond a reasonable doubt that the defendant is guilty of a particular crime. This instrument is specifically designed to protect the innocent, rather than obtain convictions (Anderson, 2005; Givelber, 2005). Under such an impartial system, is it not a virtual guarantee that only the wicked shall suffer? Unfortunately, the judicial process has been plagued by eyewitness misidentification, unfounded and improper forensic science, false confessions, substandard lawyering, and governmental misconduct leading to myriad wrongful criminal convictions (Rattner, 1988). Such revelations gnaw at the delicate social fabric of democratic republicanism.

The American criminal justice system is based on the concept that wrongs have causes, that such causes are preventable, and that injurious acts warrant recompense to victims as well as punishment for offenders (Leo & Gould, 2009). If the problem is to be addressed and rectified, it must first be understood; not as it is perceived, but as it is. The relationship between wrongful convictions and legal procedure is not one of simple cause and effect. Rather, this problem represents a dynamic interaction between defendants and observers wherein all parties play an active role. However, the wrongful conviction trend has only been subjectively accepted by the general public to any measurable degree within the past two decades (Huff, 2002).

A U.S. History of Wrongful Conviction

Judge Learned Hand said in 1923 that the American judicial system "has always been haunted by the ghost of the innocent man convicted." He referred to the notion of wrongful conviction as an "unreal dream" (Halsted, 1992; Huff, Rattner, Sagarin, & MacNamara, 1986). Serious study of this phenomenon began less than a decade after the judge made his innocuous statements. Contrary to his honor's eloquent rhetoric, time and technology have revealed that an unquantifiable number of wrongfully convicted persons have served prison sentences and even been executed for crimes which were committed by others and even some that never occurred (Huff, 2002).

It is difficult to articulate the wrongful conviction trend and determine the growth or recession of the problem. This is due to the unavoidable fact that a wrongful conviction can only be unequivocally known to have taken place if the offender has been subsequently exonerated by the same system which was responsible for the initial error. Indeed, an appellate verdict of "not guilty" does not inherently translate to innocence (Huff, 2002).

Research into wrongful convictions was virtually nonexistent until Professor Edward Borchard of Yale University published his book *Convicting the Innocent* in 1932, which documented 65 such cases, addressed the legal causes of miscarriage, and offered suggestions for reform. In subsequent decades, numerous researchers conducted case studies and published findings which affirmed that wrongful conviction represented a systematic problem within the American judicial process. Nonetheless, legislators, law enforcement professionals, and the general public remained unconvinced and blissfully ignorant for quite some time.

The contemporary innocence revolution began with an article published by Bedau and Radelet in 1987. Therein, 350 wrongful convictions, 23 of which had led to executions, were identified and exposed (Leo & Gould, 2009). The public was immediately aroused and haunted by the notion that the "unreal dream" of the innocent man convicted was a harsh reality. These revelations ushered in the modern history of miscarriages of justice.

The introduction of DNA testing to the courtroom has certainly elevated the issue in public discourse. Gary Dotson became the first prisoner to be exonerated by post-conviction DNA evidence in 1989. This landmark case initiated the movement which has been responsible for overturning more than 300 convictions to date. Once assumed to be a preposterous notion, 94 percent of recent poll respondents believed that innocent defendants are sometimes executed via the American judicial process (Gould & Leo, 2010; Leo, 2005). Unfortunately, researchers will likely never know exactly how many innocent defendants have lost their lives, or the better part of them, due to miscarriages of justice (Zalman, Larson, & Smith, 2012).

In 2000, then-Governor George Ryan imposed a moratorium on the death penalty in the State of Illinois and expressed his outrage toward a flawed system wherein more death row inmates had been exonerated than executed (Leo, 2005). Shortly thereafter, U.S. Senator Patrick Leahy introduced the Innocence Protection Act and proclaimed that miscarriages of justice come at a high social cost. Public confidence in the judicial system is undermined, innocent people suffer, and public safety is compromised because for every person wrongfully convicted there is a real criminal who may still be roaming the streets (Blackerby, 2003; Zalman, 2006).

Contemporary estimates contend that perhaps as many as 7,500 persons arrested for index crimes are wrongfully convicted annually in the United States, though there are no extant reliable statistics on the precise incidence of miscarriages of justice (Huff, 2002; Zalman, Larson, & Smith, 2012). Currently, the factual rate of wrongful conviction is believed to be as high as 5 percent in rape-murder cases (Gould & Leo, 2010; Risinger, 2007). However, similar figures on crimes which traditionally produce less forensic evidence remain elusive. Nonetheless, many researchers contend that recent case studies have only revealed the tip of the proverbial iceberg (Huff, 2002). Scholars can hardly trend the history and state of these miscarriages as modern developments in DNA technology have been largely responsible for their identification through post-conviction exonerations. Though, the issue is certainly perceived as worsening since innocent people have recently been exonerated in droves (Krieger, 2011). A recent survey study conducted by Zalman, Larson, and Smith (2012) revealed that the vast majority of citizens believed that wrongful convictions occur at least occasionally (55%) or frequently (20%).

The United States houses the largest national prison population in the world with over nine million offenders under some form of correctional supervision. This behemoth of a custodial system arrived at this nearly incomprehensible figure following a four-fold prison population explosion which began in the 1980s; the same decade which saw the birth of the modern innocence revolution (Schmalleger & Smykla, 2009, p. 5). Much of this growth is attributable to zealous enforcement of "War on Drugs" policies which, however well-intentioned, have simultaneously criminalized non-violent offenses and increased the likelihood of wrongful conviction (Halsted, 1992).

Notably, the national clearance rate for murder was over 90 percent in 1960. In subsequent decades, the rate of homicides cleared by arrest or exceptional means gradually declined to just over 60 percent by 2010. Paradoxically, clearance rates for murder in metropolitan statistical areas have declined almost perpetually with no demonstrable improvement for over half a century; a trend which is not attributable to the documented increases in police workloads (Ousey & Lee, 2010). A plausible contributor to this decline in clearance rates is that advancements in DNA and forensic technologies have added to the weight of the State's burden of proof in serious felony cases, as indicated by the fact that law enforcement professionals have actually cleared proportionally fewer murders and forcible rapes than when DNA databases were in their infancy (Rothstein & Talbott, 2006). Post-conviction exonerations do not affect these data since an arrest is sufficient to clear a case according to the Uniform Crime Reports (U.S. Department of Justice: Federal Bureau of Investigation, 2011). Thereby, it can be ascertained that the current legal system, which is demonstrably incapable of operating with complete accuracy, has been unable to sufficiently secure convictions using scientific evidence in cases which may have otherwise resulted in miscarriages.

Ostensibly, the data convey that the justice system operates with a very small margin of error. Indeed, a few hundred miscarriages do not seem to represent a major social problem when compared to a prison community equivalent to the population of Hong Kong, China (U.S. Department of State, 2011). However, this façade of precision is merely the byproduct of historic public faith in the system and resultant indifference toward convicted offenders. The decline in national clearance rates serves as evidence that jury members are no longer content to make decisions in the absence of DNA and forensic data. Indeed, scientific experimentation has affirmed that historical clearance rates were most likely the inflated and fictitious remnants of an era before technology entered the courtroom (Rothstein & Talbott, 2006). Therefore, wrongful convictions are not aberrations, but consequences of the normal operations of a flawed system (Siegel, 2005). Consequently, nearly every U.S. state has adopted a legal statute which allows access to post-conviction DNA testing (Steinback, 2007).

An Interactionist Perspective

Labeling theory proposes that acts are not inherently criminal. Rather, criminality is determined by the audience which labels the person and his or her acts (Leon-Guerrero, 2011, p. 347). Accordingly, deviance is largely determined by the cognitive representations harbored by observers. Prior to the advent of modern forensics, convictions weighed heavily on eyewitness testimony and other fallible factors.

Jackiw, Arbuthnott, Pfeifer, Marcon, and Meissner (2008) analyzed the first 130 cases of post-conviction DNA exoneration. Therein, they affirmed that 78 percent of the original wrongful convictions had resulted wholly or in part from mistaken eyewitness identification. Accordingly, they concluded that observers' recollections of events are often inaccurate and incomplete. Very often, these memories are formed out of an informal reasoning fallacy, the argument from ignorance, as the observers' minds attempt to make sense of the events by simply filling in what "probably" happened in accordance with their own preconceived notions; especially concerning members of minority groups identified by Caucasian witnesses and victims (Oaksford & Hahn, 2004). The cross-racial misidentification phenomenon is at least partially responsible for the trend in exonerations of minority defendants in felony cases (Aaronson, 2008).

As with many social problems, particularly those concerning the justice process, race is an omnipresent factor in wrongful conviction. Scholars have speculated that African-Americans are disproportionally targeted by the criminal justice system (Taslitz, 2006; Zalman, Larson, & Smith, 2012). For instance, nearly 90 percent of offenders executed for rape convictions since 1930 were African-American. Prosecutors are also more likely to move forward with comparably weak cases against non-Caucasian defendants. Consequently, minority defendants are often convicted for having killed Caucasian victims based on significantly less evidence than in similar cases with Caucasians defendant. As a result, six times more African-Americans have been exonerated from capital sentences than Caucasians;

indicating that African-Americans are far more likely to be wrongfully convicted during their initial trials.

Given that African-Americans make up 13 percent of the United States' population and one-third of its prison community, but are wrongfully convicted at such a staggering rate, labeling theory suggests that the majority of individuals involved in capital trials may perceive minorities as being more deviant (Harmon, 2004). The findings from Chambliss' (1973) classic "The Saints and the Roughnecks" certainly apply herein. Caucasians in this instance are more resistant to the criminal label than are minorities (Leon-Guerrero, 2011, p. 347).

Undoubtedly, socio-economic status is inextricably linked to racial inequality as over one-fourth of the African-American community lives in poverty (Leon-Guerrero, 2011, p. 44; U.S. Census Bureau, 2011). As noted by Crone (2011), one consequence of this disparity is that those in higher social classes benefit from an increasing number of opportunities, such as private attorneys (p.55). Accordingly, researchers have affirmed that the use of public or private defenders plays a significant role in miscarriages of justice (Blackerby, 2003; Gould & Leo, 2010; Huff, 2004).

Identifying Causes and Proposing Solutions

Though media attention has dwindled in recent years, most criminal justice professionals are conscious of the wrongful conviction trend. Moreover, recent documentaries and television series have launched the issue into the public eye (Campbell & Denov, 2004). Policy makers have been berated with demands for improved legislation and oversight, particularly regarding capital cases, while advocacy agencies have pushed for the forensic re-examination of cases which were decided before the technology became available;

which has led to a substantial backlog of defendants (Siegel, 2005). Since the fairness of our judicial system is often taken for granted, wrongful conviction may soon be subjectively perceived as a threat to our cherished legal institution without timely intervention.

Previous research has identified the root causes of wrongful conviction as well as its purpose. From where did this trend emerge? Miscarriages are the result of ill-planned "tough on crime" initiatives advocated by politicians in their quest to appease the masses and public trust in the equitable delivery of justice. Subsequently, courtroom actors neglected the State's burden of proof in favor of erring on the side of caution and ultimately, though unwittingly, opened the door to misconduct (Rattner, 1988). Moreover, the disproportional treatment of minorities is evidence that the civil rights movement has not yet reached the top of the mountain; bias remains in the courtroom (Harmon, 2004; Taslitz, 2006). What function does this problem serve? Contemporary juries now come to court with high expectations regarding DNA and forensic evidence. The initial surge of post-conviction exonerations is nearing its end, though it has revealed systematic flaws in the judicial process which have been ignored for decades (Bowman, 2008).

Eyewitness misidentification has been identified as the most prevalent cause of wrongful conviction (Clark & Godfrey, 2009; Rattner, 1988). Notably, a misidentification can result in the wrongful conviction of an innocent person as well as prompt police investigators to stop looking for the real offender. Theoretical analyses into eyewitness memory and identification have mostly been conducted by social and cognitive psychologists (Leo, 2005). Nonetheless, criminal justice professionals have learned practical lessons from these data. For instance, the use of double-blind lineup procedures was first mandated by the State of New Jersey and has since been adopted by numerous, though not most, law enforcement agencies. Therein, the officer administering the lineup does not know the identity of the suspect.

Additionally, sequential photo arrays, wherein each photo is shown one time to prevent comparative analyses, have been implemented as a best practice (Garrett, 2012). Moreover, Weber and Perfect (2012) affirmed that free-report decisions made by witnesses were most accurate, especially when an explicit "don't know" option was permitted, and had no negative influence on the number of correct decisions. Therefore, witnesses should be informed that the guilty party may not be present in the lineup and that they are not required to answer definitively when presented with suspects for identification. The results, to include the witnesses' certainty at the time of identification should be recorded. Additionally, model jury instructions should direct jurors not to rely solely on the "confidence level" of any eyewitness in the absence of more convincing evidence (Garrett, 2012). If these procedures are followed, eyewitness identifications will be much more reliable and remove ambiguity at trial. This simultaneously reduces the likelihood of wrongful conviction and improves the overall cogency of the State's case.

A confession is arguably the most damaging evidence that can be brought against a defendant in a court of law. Ostensibly, it seems reasonable to assume that one would only confess to a crime that he or she had actually committed. However, in the United States, false confessions may result in nearly 400 wrongful felony convictions annually (Cassell, 1998). Leo (2005) affirmed that false confessions, to include guilty pleas, were present in 25 percent of wrongful conviction cases. Notably, such confessions were disproportionately concentrated in cases of serious violent crime and capital offenses.

A full two-thirds of post-conviction DNA exoneration homicide cases involved false confessions. In eight such cases, false confessions resulted in conviction despite exclusionary forensic evidence presented at the trials. One is compelled to question the differences in interrogation methods utilized by investigators according to the severity of the crime. In numerous wrongful convictions, the defendants were mentally ill and/or juveniles. Many were interrogated for several hours and reported being threatened or physically coerced by investigators (Garrett, 2012).

Nonetheless, this pervasive contributor to wrongful convictions can be easily remedied. Most importantly, all interrogations should be recorded in their entirety to improve the reliability of confessions as evidence (Huff, 2002). Over 750 law enforcement agencies have adopted this practice voluntarily. Prosecutors and investigators often welcome such policy changes as they generally result in fewer motions to suppress and reduce claims of abuse. Provided that these recordings are reviewed by a judge prior to trial, this practice protects the innocent and aids in prosecution (Garrett, 2012).

The criminal justice system is comprised of individuals who are incentivized by their own personal responsibilities and goals which can conflict with those of other actors within the system. Consequently, post-conviction exonerations have exposed unethical behavior at every stage of the judicial process (Huff, 2002; Rattner, 1988). Accordingly, it would be disingenuous to address the wrongful conviction phenomenon whilst ignoring the prevalence of governmental misconduct. Police investigators have repeatedly been found to have coerced confessions and witness identifications, mislead jurors regarding their observations, intentionally withheld exculpatory evidence from prosecutors, and provided compensation to informants for unreliable evidence. Similarly, state prosecutors have mishandled or destroyed evidence as well as withheld it from the defense, pressured witnesses, and relied on fraudulent forensic "experts" whose opinions were based on compensation (Garrett, 2012; Gould & Leo, 2010).

This behavior, while abhorrent, is likely to continue unless legislators can overcome a fundamental problem; investigators and prosecutors are generally rewarded based upon the number of cases solved and convictions obtained. Viable quality assurance measures must be adopted in order to ensure the accuracy of investigations in identifying the guilty (Gould & Leo, 2010; Martin, 1998). Moreover, real consequences must be implemented for those who engage in misconduct (Gould, 2008). Anyone shown to have knowingly or recklessly contributed to the conviction of an innocent person should be subject to a legal public response. Potential repercussions should include the revocation of attorneys' licenses to practice and law enforcement officials' peace officer certifications in addition to criminal charges and/or civil suits (Huff, 2002).

Conclusion

Research conducted in the years since Bedau and Radelet's watershed study has revealed the once majestic American judicial system to be as fallible as the humans who comprise it. Previously content with presumptive faith in justice and inflated clearance rates, legal professionals have acknowledged the necessity for reform within this cherished institution. Legislators and politicians have largely accepted the empirically-supported criticism and adopted policies which aim to prevent miscarriages of justice.

Technology has afforded us the opportunity to identify systematic flaws and reduce the negative impact of the human errors that contribute to wrongful conviction; such as eyewitness misidentification, false confessions, and misconduct. Additional miscarriages will undoubtedly be revealed in the future as advocacy agencies continue to represent and support the innocent. Simultaneously, local and state governments, along with law enforcement agencies, should continue to embrace improved lineup, interrogation, and evidence handling procedures. This process promises to be wrought with humbling and uncomfortable revelations as more inadequacies are brought to light. Eventually, the innocent man convicted will become a rarity in the American justice system.

II

Evaluating the Impact of "Three Strikes" Laws on Crime Rates and Prison Populations in California and Washington

Three strikes laws gained national popularity with the landmark passage of California's "Three Strikes and You're Out" sentencing guidelines in 1994. Subsequently, the federal government and most U.S. states have enacted or augmented applicable mandatory sentencing laws and habitual offender statutes (Dickey & Hollenhorst, 1999). Ostensibly, early reductions in overall crime rates served as justification for three strikes advocates. However, many researchers attribute much of the phenomenon to preexisting trends independent of legislation, asserting that a comprehensive decline was observed in the 1990s throughout North America (Eskridge, 2004, p. 15-23).

Regardless, early research studies were only able to analyze month-to-month trends and were largely confined to samples in one state (Stolzenberg & D'Alessio, 1997). Now that sufficient time has passed since the first three strikes law was implemented, more detailed longitudinal analyses have been published. Recent studies have indicated that these laws have not yielded results consistent with the initial hype. Nonetheless, three strikes legislation appears to have modestly influenced crime reductions in some states (Kelly & Datta, 2009).

The rationale behind the passage of three strikes legislation by the U.S. Congress and over half of the individual states was that mandatory sentencing punishments would effectively deter criminals and protect the general public from those repeat offenders who remain unimpeded by amassing the convicted into the penal system under weighty prison terms (Peak 2010, p. 312). However, Austin, Clark, Hardyman, and Henry (1999) contended that the legislation was actually drafted to be primarily symbolic in nature with little practicality, citing that previously existing crime prevention methods had already been employed by all of the three strikes states.

As shown in Table 1, most three strikes states intentionally adopted a minimalist approach to the application of these laws. Accordingly, much of the initial governmental and academic scrutiny of mandatory sentencing focused on California's zealous enforcement and not necessarily on the "striking out" concept itself (Chen, 2008). Critics argued that formidable mandatory sentences would bombard the courts with defendants who refused to plea bargain in favor of a trial by jury; thus burdening the legal system with excessive case loads, hindering its ability to facilitate speedy trials, and raising court costs to the state. Moreover, they contended that imposing lengthy sentences would prompt an increase in prison populations within already overpopulated facilities (Willis, 2007). Ergo, a series of decisions made by legislators had the potential to reverberate across the entire criminal justice system and into local communities.

Table 1. Use of Three Strikes Laws by State

Jurisdiction	Year Law Enacted	Number of Convictions	Data Current as of
Alaska	1996	1	8/98
Arkansas	1995	12	8/98
California	1994	40,511	7/98
Colorado	1994	2	8/98
Connecticut	1994	1	8/98
Florida	1995	116	6/98
Georgia	1994	942	3/98
Indiana	1994	38	7/98
Maryland	1994	5	12/97
Montana	1995	0	8/98
Nevada	1995	304	8/98
New Jersey	1995	6	8/98
New Mexico	1994	1	8/98
N. Carolina	1994	5	12/97
Pennsylvania	1995	3	12/96
S. Carolina	1995	825	10/97
Tennessee	1994	5	7/98
Utah	1995	0	8/98
Vermont	1995	4	8/98
Virginia	1994	0	8/98
Washington	1993	121	8/98
Wisconsin	1994	3	8/98
Federal	1994	35	10/97

*Kansas, Louisiana, and North Dakota excluded due to lack of data

Crime Rates in California and Washington

The State of California enacted the nation's most infamous and farthest-reaching three strikes law. Therein, a mandatory sentence of 25 years to life in prison was established for any repeat offender convicted of three qualifying felonies. The most notable component of California's habitual offender statute, contrary to most other states' laws, is that qualifying felonies are not relegated to violent crimes alone. Ergo, it is markedly more punitive than most. Under the second-strike provision, if an offender has a prior serious or violent felony conviction, the sentence for a subsequent felony is automatically doubled. Similarly, a third felony conviction thereafter results in a third-strike sentence of 25 years to life (Willis, 2007).

Ultimately, more than 60 separate felony offenses are regarded as strikes under California law. By 2005, the broad nature of the statute was responsible for over 87,500 second- and third-strike convictions (Chen, 2008). Figure 1 illustrates the three strikes rate in California juxtaposed against the average rate for 21 other three strikes states (Schiraldi, Colburn, & Lotke, 2004, p. 6). These results convey that California's habitual offender statute is demonstrably unique and rampantly employed.

Figure 1. Three Strikes Rates per 100,000 Citizens

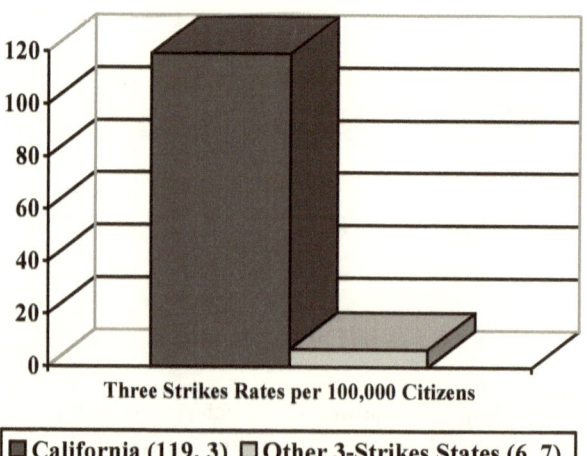

Three Strikes Rates per 100,000 Citizens

■ California (119. 3) ☐ Other 3-Strikes States (6. 7)

The shear scope of the law's applicability has produced significant monetary cost to the State's taxpayers. Studies conducted prior to the enactment of the California mandatory sentencing guidelines projected a 25 percent crime reduction at an annual cost of $5.5 billion if the law were fully implemented, which it was not (Meehan, 2000). Subsequently, between 1994 and 1997, the total crime rate in California dropped by 20.2 percent with a 13.8 percent reduction in violent crime. However, a 1999 Justice Policy Institute study concluded that the reduction was in no way attributed to three strikes law because crime rates had already started to decline in other regions of the United States prior to the law's implementation and declared that California's mandatory sentencing legislation was a failure (Chen, 2008).

Compared to California's mandatory sentencing legislation, The State of Washington's simple and comprehensible Initiative 593 is narrower in scope and far less punitive (Caulkins, 2001). Therein, anyone tried as an adult and convicted of three serious felonies on separate occasions receives a mandatory sentence of life in prison without the possibility of parole. Notably, spree offenses are counted as a single strike since the aim of the law is to incapacitate dangerous repeat offenders and distinguish their transgressions from crimes of passion. Unlike the California three strikes law which permits ample discretion by judges and allows them to dismiss prior strikes, only the Governor may grant a pardon or clemency under Initiative 593.

One axiomatic distinction of Washington's mandatory sentencing law is that only serious felony crimes such as murder, rape, assault, child molestation, and robbery are regarded as strikes. Thereby, only the most egregious 12 percent of the State's felonies qualify under its three strikes law (LaCourse, 1994). Initiative 593 targets violent repeat offenders since research has affirmed that a meager seven percent of the criminal population is responsible for over half of all violent crimes; to include three-quarters of rapes and robberies as well as almost all murders (Jennings 2006). Notably, the likelihood of recidivism into violent crime for a released third-striker is 76 percent. Hence, Initiative 593 is specifically applicable to this minute, albeit actively contributing, portion of the criminal population so as to impose the strictest penalty possible, sans execution, upon the most dangerous repeat offenders (LaCourse, 1994).

Given the narrow scope of Initiative 593, significant reductions in crime rates were not expected since the law, by design, applies to relatively few offenders (Dickey & Hollenhorst, 1999). However, within four months following its implementation, a dozen violent criminals; rapists, assaulters, child molesters, and robbers, each with several prior convictions who generally preyed on women and the elderly, were sentenced to life in prison. Notably, one of these offenders, Michael Johnson, was actually a fourth-striker, since he had committed three prior felonies before 1993. His final conviction was the result of his decision to kidnap and repeatedly rape a 16 year-old girl at knifepoint.

Unfortunately, multiple violent felony offenses are not uncommon for repeat criminals like Johnson. Larry Fisher was also sentenced under Initiative 593 following his commission of an armed robbery which became his 17th conviction; six of which were felonies (LaCourse, 1994). Within five years of the law's enactment, nearly half of all offenders serving life without parole in Washington were third-strikers (Dickey & Hollenhorst, 1999). In hindsight, perhaps the only regret attached to Initiative 593 is that earlier passage may have prevented several rapes, robberies, and assaults in the State of Washington.

Impact on National Crime Trends

Chen (2008) analyzed state-level crime data for the entire United States, with particular attention paid to three strikes states, from 1986 to 2005 in order to quantify the efficacy of the legislation pursuant to deterrence and incapacitation. Therein, seven separate offenses were trended; murder and non-negligent manslaughter, forcible rape, robbery, aggravated assault, burglary, larceny/theft, and motor vehicle theft. The primary purpose of the study was to determine the impact of other three strikes states' laws as compared to California's. This was done in order to discern which variations of the legislation had produced the most significant results. Theoretically, the California law would have had a greater impact on crime rates than did comparable laws in other states given its scope and frequency of application. Moreover, rates for instrumental crimes (e.g. burglary, larceny) should have fallen more dramatically, considering that these crimes generally involve more forethought and could be more easily deterred.

An evaluation of the data revealed that three strikes states experienced a slower decline in most areas of crime prior to the implementation of their laws when compared to other states, which may have been responsible for the laws' initial gravitas among citizens and policy-makers. Interestingly, murder rates in three strikes states declined 12.9 percent less rapidly than the national trend, indicating that the fear of mandatory sentencing may have motivated certain criminals to eliminate witnesses and visit violence upon arresting officers (Chen, 2008). Nonetheless, this trend was not especially pronounced in California as would have been expected (Johnson & Saint-Germain, 2005).

Figure 2. UCR Index Crime Offense Rates for Cities with 100,000+ Population (1980-2000)

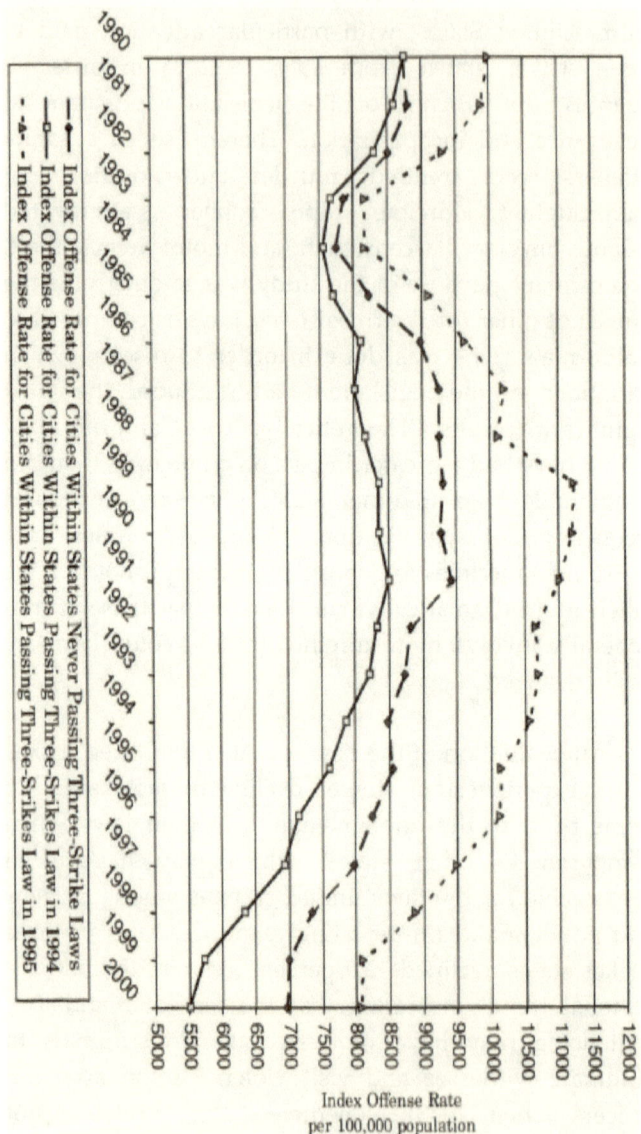

Index Offense Rate
per 100,000 population

Additionally, crime rates for instrumental offenses fell annually at rates ranging from about 1 to 3 percent more rapidly in three strikes states when adjusted for the preexisting nationwide crime rate reduction trend. However, this cannot be attributed comprehensively to the legislation since these crimes are not covered under most states' three strikes provisions. Accordingly, few statistically significant declines and no additional incapacitation effects were observed for instrumental crimes in three strikes states (Chen, 2008). Moreover, in their analysis of 188 metropolitan statistical areas, Kovandzic, Sloan, and Vieraitis (2004) affirmed that cities in three strikes states did not experience any significant reductions in crime rates independent of the national trend as illustrated in Figure 2.

Impact on Prison Populations

In the past three decades, the American custodial system has expanded by over 400 percent following a period of stability which had survived for more than half a century as shown in Figure 3. The United States currently houses 25 percent of the global prison population with over two million inmates and nearly seven million parolees and probationers (Gottschalk, 2006). Collectively, states currently spend approximately $43 billion on corrections annually (Pfaff, 2008). Nevertheless, it is 17 times more expensive for a society to have high-rate repeat offenders on the street rather than incarcerated (LaCourse, 1994). This is representative not only of how American society regards its marginalized citizens, but of how its governing bodies allocate financial resources and respond to paradigm shifts in crime and social disorder (Pfaff, 2008). It was in response to such a shift, in the middle of the prison population explosion, that three strikes laws were first adopted.

Figure 3. United States Prison Population (1925-2004)

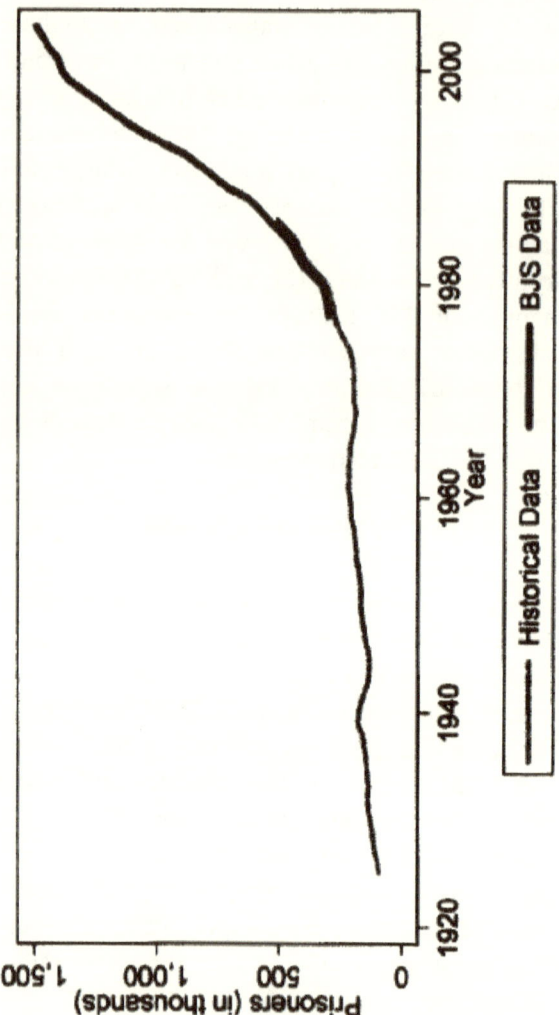

Between 1984 and 1994, the California prison system received a more than 200 percent increase in funding. During that time, the State erected 21 new prisons (Irwin, Schiraldi, & Ziedenberg, 2000). Notably, this asset reallocation occurred prior to the enactment of the State's three strikes law and was necessitated by the nationwide prison population explosion. Mandatory sentencing is projected to cost California taxpayers about $16,300 annually at the correctional level per serious crime prevented (Meehan, 2000). By 2008, California had imprisoned more than 250 times the number of offenders under mandatory sentencing law than any other three strikes state (Chen, 2008).

Due to constraints on population growth in already grossly overpopulated facilities, entry into the correctional system by inmates with mandatory sentences could only be facilitated if other inmates were released. Thereby, incapacitation effects would materialize only if the paroled offenders were less likely to commit crimes than those who are incarcerated under three strikes law. Consequently, some researchers have contended that the disproportional representation of nonviolent offenders in the California prison population is attributable to mandatory sentencing (Meehan, 2000). Indeed, the nonviolent prisoner population therein has grown exponentially since 1980. However, Table 2 shows that drug offenders account for a significant portion of the expansion. Therefore, the increasing prevalence of nonviolent offenders in the California custodial system may be influenced primarily by federal War on Drugs policies and not directly related to three strikes law (Auerhahn, 2004).

Table 2. California Prison Population (1980-1998)

Year	Prison Population	Drug Prison Population	Percent Drug
1980	20,248	1,967	10%
1985	52,841	11,232	21%
1990	94,161	26,652	28%
1995	136,179	41,578	31%
1998	155,888	50,099	32%

Moreover, if incarceration of the prophesized influx of strikers had necessitated the release of current prisoners, the trend should be identifiable in California's parolee population. If critics were correct in their presumptions, the number of parolees therein should have increased noticeably through the late-1990s following the enactment of the State's habitual offender statute. However, Figure 4 shows that this projected expansion has not taken place.

The most dramatic rises in parolee releases occurred prior to the passage of California's three strikes law in 1994. Parolee population increases ranging from 6 to 12 percent were observed in subsequent years before entering into a three-year period of stability beginning in 1999 which was followed by two consecutive years of decline; -7 percent in 2002 and -2 percent in 2003 (California Department of Corrections and Rehabilitation, 2008, 8a). These data convey that three strikes law has not directly influenced parolee population statistics in California even though a significant number of strikers have been incarcerated.

Figure 4. Total Felon Releases to Parole in California

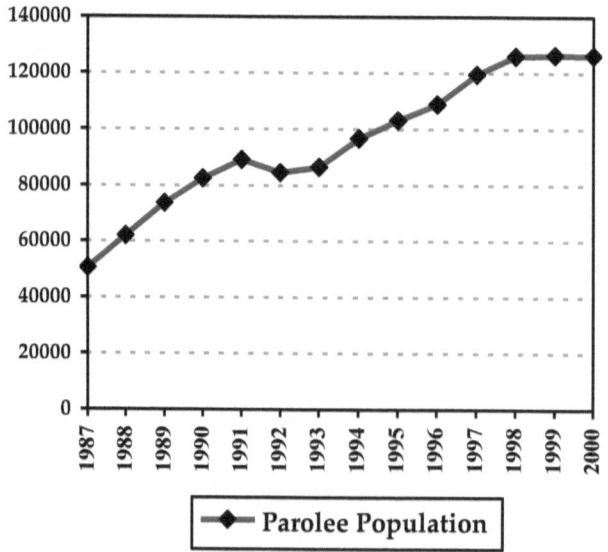

Washington has also not experienced a significantly increased burden on correctional facilities or taxpayers as a result of mandatory sentencing, perhaps partially due to infrequent employment of Initiative 593. The State's prison population was expected to grow by 9 percent over a 20-year period. However, even this manageable figure was not met in the first year and future estimates were lowered accordingly (LaCourse, 1994). Using data provided by the Washington State Department of Corrections (2012), Figure 5 illustrates the relatively stable growth of the State's prison population. Notably, no significant increase independent of the existing trend was observed following the State's enactment of three strikes law in December of 1993 or after the passage a separate two-strike provision in 1996.

Figure 5. Washington State Prison Population

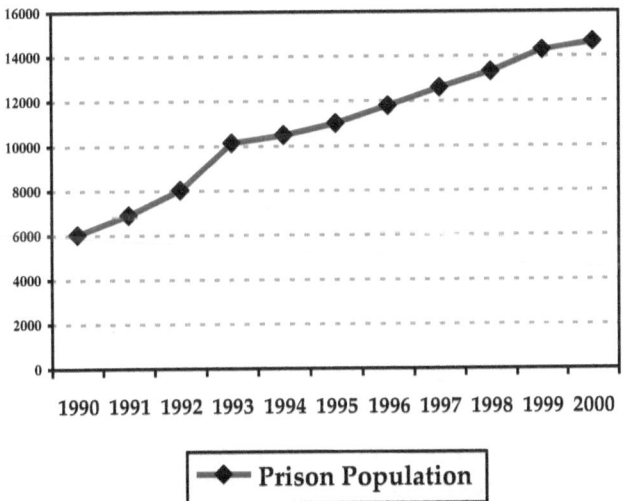

An unanticipated consequence of the Washington's three strikes law, given its narrow scope, was its significant deterrence effect. Instances of rape, robbery, and aggravated assault have declined noticeably (Dickey & Hollenhorst, 1999). Law enforcement, legal, and corrections professionals have stated that many current and former inmates have expressed concern and requested information such as which crimes are covered by three strikes law. Moreover, a subsequent micro-exodus of criminals has resulted. Numerous second-strikers, particularly sex offenders, have relocated outside of the State since 1993. Many of those second-strike offenders who remained voluntarily sought treatment and enrolled in rehabilitation programs, some at their own expense, immediately after Initiative 593 went into effect (LaCourse, 1994). It is apparent that Washington's mandatory sentencing guidelines have produced a strong deterrence effect and have the potential to compel repeat offenders to reconsider their lives of crime. Some of those who have not been deterred have decided to relocate, which substantiates the efficacy of Initiative 593 within the borders of the State of Washington.

When the first three strikes statutes were enacted, opponents argued that prison systems would be overwhelmed with resultant population increases. However, the number of offenders sentenced during the first three years of Washington's legislation was actually 63 percent lower than the maximum expectation. Moreover, mandatory sentencing data compelled corrections officials in California to lower their five year incarceration projections by 40,000 inmates. The dismal figures proposed by early critics have not been realized because most three strikes laws target violent repeat offenders who were already receiving lengthy prison terms under existing legislation (Gatland, 1998).

Public Perception of Three Strikes

Regardless of arrest and crime reduction statistics, citizens often cite crime as their primary concern when randomly polled. Most often, repeat violent and sex offenders garner the most fear among the citizenry even at times when crime rates for these offenses are down. This public fear was largely responsible for the romanticized promises which ultimately materialized into mandatory sentencing laws in the 1990s (Dickey & Hollenhorst, 1999). Fear of crime can also be attributed to the victims' movement, which brought violent and sex crimes into the public eye and rekindled the case for restorative justice. Unlike in the past, contemporary victims of violent crime have come forward to express their personal suffering and bring attention to a formerly abstract social problem. In order to appease the masses, law makers across the United States were compelled to implement three strikes laws; most aimed specifically at violent and sex offenders (Berliner, 1994).

Neither California nor Washington experienced dramatic reductions in crime rates; though for different reasons respectively. The recognizable difference observed following the passage of mandatory sentencing legislation has been public perception, even though both initiatives were originally passed by large voter margins. The Justice Policy Institute has recommended that California abandon or significantly modify its three strikes policy due to budget concerns and lack of positive outcomes (Schiraldi, Colburn, & Lotke, 2004). Subsequently, a ballot initiative and state Senate bill were introduced which aimed to bring California's mandatory sentencing guidelines more in line with those of other states by reducing the number of crimes regarded as qualifying felonies; both failed at the polls partially due to a multi-million dollar gubernatorial-sponsored media campaign (Chen, 2008).

Contrarily, Initiative 593 has been largely embraced by the public. The Washington media has covered stories wherein inmates proclaimed their fear of "Three Strikes and You're Out" (LaCourse, 1994). Thereby, citizens felt that their communities were being protected by mandatory sentencing legislation, even though it had not produced an overwhelming reduction in violent crime rates. Perhaps, the honesty of Washington politicians regarding the limited applicability and realistic expectations of three strikes in their state is also responsible for the resultant public support. Moreover, Washington law makers proved to their constituents that Initiative 593 has been cost-effective; which their counterparts in California were unable to accomplish (Dickey & Hollenhorst, 1999). Three strikes law in Washington has improved public perception of the criminal justice system even in the absence of impressive crime reduction statistics.

Conclusion and Reflection

The efficacy of three strikes laws has been a topic of contention among criminal justice practitioners and researchers since the first such piece of legislation was implemented in the United States nearly two decades ago. Chen (2008) concluded that crime rates in three strikes states had declined slower than the national average prior to their laws' enactment. The resultant public fear of crime prompted a legislative response via mandatory sentencing guidelines (Berliner, 1994). Nonetheless, states which have implemented three strikes laws have not experienced reductions in violent crime rates to any greater extent than those with no such legislation (Kovandzic, Sloan, & Vieraitis, 2004).

The opposition's expectation of a prison population explosion has not materialized. Three strikes states have not suffered a noticeable increase in incarceration rates subsequent to the implementation of mandatory sentencing laws as predicted by critics (Gatland, 1998). Even in states where three strikes was expected to have a major impact, projections were unfounded and very little impact has been felt directly by the courts and corrections systems in most jurisdictions (Austin, Clark, Hardyman, & Henry, 1999). Some researchers contend that the disproportionate representation of nonviolent offenders within the California prison population may compromise the long-term cogency of mandatory sentencing (Irwin, Schiraldi, & Ziedenberg, 2000). However, the expansion of this prisoner demographic does not appear to have been directly caused by three strikes law and may be better explained through evaluations of existing War on Drugs initiatives (Auerhahn, 2004).

Although the limited applicability of most states' mandatory sentencing guidelines is unlikely to produce significant incapacitation and deterrence effects, Washington has demonstrated that such legislation can effectively target violent repeat offenders and reduce fear of crime (LaCourse, 1994). Additionally, properly tailored three strikes laws have had a demonstrable impact on instrumental crimes over time. It seems plausible that this effect could be the result of residual deterrence as offenders become less certain as to the likelihood of apprehension and increasingly fearful of mandatory sentencing (Chen 2008). This popular legislative response to crime is in need of revision concerning the scope of crimes regarded as qualifying felonies in some jurisdictions, particularly California. The broad-brush approach to violent crime has proven wholly ineffective. An efficacious legislative response must be necessarily targeted upon violent repeat offenders in order to legitimately improve public safety and reduce fear of crime.

III

A Multi-State Analysis of Correctional Boot Camp Outcomes: Identifying Vocational Rehabilitation as a Complement to Shock Incarceration

The goal of most contemporary justice programs is to reduce recidivism rates and curb prison overcrowding. However, incarceration is an expensive form of punishment which has not produced any promising results via rearrest statistics or budget projections. Consequently, legislators and corrections administrators have been forced to seek alternatives through intermediate and non-custodial sanctions (Bhati & Piquero, 2007; Stincomb, 1999). Success therein would subsequently reduce costs and mediate the monetary burden on the justice system inherent to the "revolving door" paradigm.

The concept of diversion was born out labeling theory and the inherent realization that incarceration can do more harm than good regarding offender rehabilitation. Proponents favor various forms of therapy, counseling, and educational programs which aim to either keep offenders out of the justice system altogether or limit their penetration therein to avoid the stigmatization of being officially adjudicated and convicted. Ultimately, the objective therein is to prevent first-time offenders from becoming repeat career criminals (Davidson, Redner, Blakely, Mitchell, & Emshoff, 1987).

American juvenile correctional boot camps were created in the 1980s on the foundation of diversion ideology as a form of intermediate sanction. According to Duwe and Kerschner (2008), boot camps were initially centered on the "shock education" notion that paramilitary regimentation and physical activity could reform offenders by instilling discipline. Additionally, in an effort to combat prison overcrowding, program graduates were afforded earlier release than they would have received under a standard sentence, usually serving the remainder of their terms on supervised probation. The projected reduction in recidivism rates and prison populations spurred a nation-wide boot camp craze which resulted in the establishment of over one hundred such programs at every jurisdictional level within the United States by the mid-1990s.

With the benefit of hindsight, researchers have since been able to evaluate these programs many years after their initial luster has faded (MacKenzie, Brame, McDowall, & Souryal, 1995). Correctional boot camps seem to have produced disappointing results and many have suffered from publicized incidents of abuse at the hands of staff, leading to several closures in various states (Bottcher & Ezell, 2005; Stincomb, 1999). The proper way to ascertain the cogency of correctional boot camp programs is to juxtapose the recidivism rates of program graduates with those of comparable offenders who received other intermediate sanctions or prison sentences. In accordance with the goals of the contemporary criminal justice system, this evaluation will determine whether or not boot camps in three U.S. states have improved public safety by producing their intended effects on recidivism rates and prison populations.

Juvenile Offenders in California

According to Bottcher and Ezell (2005), the State of California implemented its version of a juvenile boot camp program, LEAD (leadership, esteem, ability, and discipline), in 1992. Two separate facilities were managed by 12 teach, advise, and counsel (TAC) officers, who served as mentors. LEAD participants were carefully selected according to the following criteria; non-serious nonviolent juvenile court commitment, minimum age of 16 (later reduced to 14), history or risk of substance abuse, informed consent, medical clearance, and Youthful Offender Parole Board (YOBP) approval. Immediate disqualifiers were also established; eligibility for special mental health programs, recent violent behavior, and non-U.S. citizenship or illegal residency.

These selection criteria ensured that only the most receptive 14 percent of the male juvenile court intake pool could enter LEAD. Nonetheless, the experiment was short-lived and quietly faded out of existence in 1997. That same year, the California Youth Authority (CYA) released experimental results regarding the LEAD program which affirmed that LEAD wards were actually more likely to be rearrested than control wards; concluding that LEAD did not reduce recidivism. However, these results were released far too early to have considered the entire preponderance of outcome data.

Considering follow-up arrest statistics provided by the California Department of Justice, Bottcher and Ezell (2005) affirmed that recidivism data was disproportionally prejudicial toward LEAD graduates. This was attributed to the fact that these participants were ordered into a comparably longer intensive parole term and were more likely to be rearrested for technicalities than control juveniles. Nonetheless, the analysis concluded that only 44 percent of LEAD graduates were subsequently arrested for new criminal offenses within the first year of release, compared to 50 percent of the control group. Moreover, 30 percent of the rearrested LEAD group had been arrested for at least one serious offense within that time, compared to 37 percent of the control group.

Second-year statistics affirmed that the LEAD group was rearrested at a rate of 60 percent, compared to 69 percent in the control group. Though the data appear promising at first glance, when all factors were taken into consideration, the rearrest and serious crime rates among both groups were hardly distinguishable. According to the "survival curves," only 8 percent of each group remained arrest-free between release and the time of the study. The only observable difference between the two groups was that LEAD participants were rearrested at a 4 percent lower rate during the first 1,000 days after release than their control group contemporaries. Beyond that time, the respective statistics for both groups were virtually identical. Essentially, the only quantifiable benefit to the CYA LEAD program was that participants were incarcerated for a comparably shorter period of time, albeit within a more expensive program.

Regardless, whatever time, effort, and funding that may have been saved was quickly sucked into the LEAD vacuum via the vessels of intensive parole, increased supervision, and aftercare programs. Resultantly, California's juvenile boot camp program was no more effective at reducing recidivism nor saving money than standard custodial sanctions. LEAD's failure can be attributed primarily to its lack of effective treatment, poorly managed and hastily drafted design, and the TAC officers' gravitation toward confrontation in lieu of mentorship in accordance with CYA directives. The root of the issue is evident in the fact that CYA has long-since fallen from its position as a progressive treatment-oriented agency and has adopted a preference for punitive measures (Harris, 2007).

Adult Boot Camp in Pennsylvania

According to Kempinen and Kurlychek (2003), the Pennsylvania State Motivational Boot Camp Program was established in 1990 as a hybrid comprised of a militaristic exercise regimen and a multi-layered rehabilitation curriculum intended to reduce prison overcrowding and recidivism. Pennsylvania's design deviated from the traditional model in that it implemented a rehabilitation program centered on education, life skills training, and cognitive-behavioral/substance abuse therapy. In order to be eligible for the six-month program, male and female adult offenders must have been sentenced to no more than two years in a state prison, under the age of 35, and not have been convicted of certain violent or major drug trafficking offenses. The sentencing judge must have recommended each candidate and the Pennsylvania Department of Corrections was given final admission approval authority. Such parameters guaranteed selective admittance into the participant pool, which produced respective graduation rates or 66 to 80 percent, even though offenders were permitted to leave voluntarily. This was particularly surprising given that participants in the Pennsylvania program were generally from among a more chronic, serious, and high-risk offender population than were admitted to most traditional boot camps.

The operational distinction within the Pennsylvania program was that it focused on individual rehabilitative needs with particular emphasis on substance abuse, relapse prevention, and anger/stress management. Of every 18-hour day (7 days per week), 2.5 hours were dedicated to group therapy sessions, often led by representatives from organizations such as Alcoholics- and Narcotics-Anonymous. Notably, the program also incorporated education and employment training as prior research had substantiated that stable employment could reduce recidivism (Kempinen & Kurlychek, 2003; Nally, Lockwood, Knutson, & Ho, 2012). Approximately 92 percent of program participants who had not previously graduated from high school received their GED during their terms in the boot camp. Those with high school diplomas participated in camp maintenance and community service projects (Kempinen & Kurlychek, 2003).

As with any correctional boot camp, traditional or not, the rate of recidivism among its graduates was the ultimate test for Pennsylvania's program (MacKenzie et al., 1995). Kempinen and Kurlychek (2003) affirmed in their study that graduates of the program were actually more likely to recidivate than the prison control group; 44 versus 39 percent. However, hidden in the recidivism data was a partial explanation. The boot camp group was 8 percent more likely to commit a technical violation while on parole, for reasons similar to those observed in California. Nonetheless, the program group received 3 percent fewer new crime convictions than the control. The authors attributed a portion of the disappointing data to the fact that young adult offenders are inherently more likely to recidivate. Notably, they affirmed that the rate of recidivism in boot camp graduates decreased proportionally to the severity of their original offenses. For example, the recidivism rate for drug offenders was 18 percent less than for property crime offenders.

Employment status was another significant factor; unemployed offenders were more than twice as likely to recidivate. While repeat offenders are inherently at a high risk for recidivism, the authors concluded that graduates of the Pennsylvania program who had prior arrest records were 71 percent less likely to reoffend when compared to those released from prison. It is important to note that program graduates were not significantly more likely to commit major parole violations even though, or perhaps because, they were under comparably greater scrutiny and supervision. Though the program did not produce demonstrable reductions in recidivism, its effect on repeat offenders was certainly encouraging. With regard to prison overcrowding, the Pennsylvania program produced admirable results. On average, a term in boot camp reduced an offender's sentence by one full year. Since boot camp graduates did not reoffend at a rate significantly higher than the control group, the program was deemed to be fiscally sound and did not expose society to any quantifiably greater risk.

House Arrest versus Boot Camp in North Carolina

Criminal justice research libraries teem with comparison evaluations of correctional boot camp programs juxtaposed against standard incarceration (MacKenzie et al., 1995). However, another viable method for determining the cogency of these programs is to compare their results with those produced by more traditional intermediate sanctions and prison alternatives (Kilgore & Meade, 2004). The United States is burdened with the world's largest prison population of over two million inmates, with nearly seven million probationers and parolees (Gottschalk, 2006). Ergo, intermediate sanctions have become a popular alternative to incarceration and provide a means to alleviate some of the strain without increasing the risk to the public. However, not all alternatives are created equal and it is the duty of research professionals to determine which programs are most efficacious.

The Intensive Motivational Program of Alternative Correctional Treatment (IMPACT) was North Carolina's version of a traditional boot camp. Its objectives were to instill self-confidence, discipline, and work ethic via an organized militaristic regimen. Program participants were male offenders ranging in age from 16 to 25 who had been convicted of misdemeanor and/or non-serious felony crimes and had not previously served more than 120 days in a correctional facility. Herein, it is obvious that those admitted into the IMPACT program were comparably lower-risk than would normally require participation in a prison alternative program. IMPACT participants conducted manual labor for seven hours per day for various government agencies and those who had not graduated from high school were afforded tutoring services. Upon successful completion of the 90-day program, graduates served the remainder of their sentences on supervised probation. Contrarily, offenders ordered to electronic house arrest (EHA) in North Carolina were confined by electronic monitoring for a period of 90 days after which time they were released as high-risk cases on regular probation (Jones & Ross, 1997).

Jones and Ross (1997) conducted a comparative evaluation of recidivism rates in North Carolina produced by EHA compared to the IMPACT program by analyzing subsequent fingerprinted arrest statistics among the offenders. They affirmed that IMPACT graduates were rearrested in dramatically lower numbers than the EHA group; 38 percent less for violent/felonious sex offenses, 44 percent less for property crimes, and 45 percent less for drug offenses. Overall, only 47 percent of IMPACT graduates had recidivated by the time of the study.

Though the data appeared to substantiate the efficacy of correctional boot camps, the researchers contended that the EHA results were likely skewed by factors which could not be accounted for in the analysis such as increased supervision, technical violations, and increases in punishable probation offenses. Moreover, the strict admission requirements for the IMPACT program essentially transformed it into a probation alternative rather than an incarceration alternative since most participants were low-risk offenders. Accordingly, the EHA population represented a comparably more high-risk pool for recidivism than that of IMPACT graduates. The recidivism rates observed in the study were influenced primarily by the types of individuals within the groups more so than by the management or operations of the respective programs.

Recidivism Reduction through Vocational Rehabilitation

Contemporary recidivism literature is commanded by studies relevant to offenders who suffer from sexual paraphilia and/or substance abuse problems as well as attempts to quantify specific and general deterrence measures believed to be associated with mandatory sentencing guidelines (Colins et al., 2011; Kunselman & Vito, 2002; Lussier & Davies, 2011). However, precious little mention is made of the relationship between offender employability and the likelihood of recidivism. Nonetheless, Hancock and Raeside (2009) concluded that employability had a statistically significant positive relationship with recidivism among 200 prisoners studied over an eight-month period following release. Further research has concluded that offending diminishes when offenders obtain and maintain employment. In short, remaining employed greatly reduces the likelihood of recidivism (Nally et al., 2012; Vennard & Hedderman, 2009).

Though previous employment intervention efforts have been successful in reducing reoffense, assistance is generally not offered to more than half of all probationers and parolees in the United States (Bridges, 1998). This demonstrates that an effective strategy has been under-employed even though the recidivism rates produced through traditional methods remain discouraging. Notably, most crimes are committed by a relatively small offender population comprised of career criminals. This fact was largely responsible for the rampant adoption and revision of mandatory sentencing laws across the United States in the mid-1990s. However, longitudinal analyses have revealed that the resultant deterrence effect was either negligible or non-extant and largely attributable to a pre-existing reduction in crime rates observed throughout North America (Chen, 2008; Eskridge, 2004, pp. 15-23).

Given that the concept of deterrence has been unable to materialize in praxis, rehabilitation and reintegration strategies must be seriously considered. If an offender is reintegrated at an early enough stage in his/her criminal career, a cumulative recidivism effect should result; as would be observed if the same offender were incapacitated via incarceration (Davidson, Jimenez, Onifade, & Hankins, 2010). The difference is that public funds are required to maintain custodial supervision of a convict, while an employed offender becomes an independent entity in the private sector. Therefore, the need for vocational rehabilitation initiatives within correctional settings is axiomatic.

The under-21 age demographic represents the most viable period for employment intervention as these offenders may be more easily diverted from their criminal paths and the resultant effects should become cumulative. Deflecting these offenders from their criminal careers would have a residual effect on overall recidivism rates as these programs would specifically target the most frequently offending group (Douglas, Epstein, & Poythress, 2008; Leschied, Austin, & Jaffe, 1988). Such a large pool of candidates also increases the odds of success, given that program administrators may be more stringent in selecting participants. As has been repeatedly affirmed in program evaluations of correctional boot camps, the selection process is the first line of defense against graduate recidivism (Bottcher & Ezell, 2005; Jones & Ross, 1997; Kempinen & Kurlychek, 2003; MacKenzie et al., 1995). Additionally, since their historic re-offense rate is so high, retrospective analyses will prove more cogent in determining the impact of the treatment protocol if a properly randomized control group can be established for comparison.

Perceived employability presents a major obstacle in the path of offenders who wish to reintegrate. Excluding persons with psychiatric or intellectual disabilities, ex-convicts are perceived by the general public as the group least likely to possess the skills and characteristics associated with employability. Such is why numerous monetary incentives are offered to employers who hire ex-prisoners and offenders under non-custodial supervision. However, research has also indicated that perceptions improve regarding offenders' ability to maintain employment after they have obtained a position. Moreover, significant improvements in perception where observed when offenders had completed some form of prerelease training (Graffam, Shinkfield, & Hardcastle, 2008). Therefore, the primary challenge is getting offenders trained and hired, while probation agencies are fully capable of supervising thereafter if needed.

Perception is also an important component in occupational functioning. A cogent program must consider how particular offenses are perceived by potential employers in order to develop an adequate selection process for participants (Nally et al., 2012).

Low qualifications and severity of criminal charges significantly influence perceived employability. For instance, applicants with misdemeanor and drug possession convictions are able to increase their perceived employability with proper qualifications. However, qualifications appear to be inadequate to improve perceptions of offenders with serious felony convictions. Therefore, employment intervention must be conducted prior to an offender's release from custody, such as during their time in a shock incarceration of correctional boot camp program. Moreover, qualifications alone are insufficient to successfully reintegrate offenders unless an advocacy group assists them in securing employment prior to release (Varghese, Hardin, Bauer, & Morgan, 2010). Coordination between probation and employment agencies is absolutely vital to overall success as similar programs have been proven effective in the past (Hancock & Raeside, 2009).

Conclusion

Reid-MacNevin (1997) argued that correctional boot camp and shock incarceration programs are merely a politically-conjured vessel by which proponents have constructed a façade of crime control. Furthermore, traditional boot camp programs utterly ignore the compendium of prior research which has suggested that deterrence-based criminal justice interventions are wholly ineffective. Social factors such as poverty, unemployment, and abuse are the root causes of disadvantage. It is this disadvantage which serves as the ultimate risk factor for criminal activity and recidivism.

Legislators and correctional administrators understand that there is little that the justice system can do to combat these social issues in an expeditious manner (Kubrin & Stewart, 2006). However, properly managed correctional boot camp programs can be equally as effective as more traditional intermediate sanctions (Jones & Ross, 1997). Through innovations in intensive treatment protocols, it is possible that these programs may eventually provide a cogent alternative to incarceration.

Contemporary evidence weighs heavily against the use of traditional discipline-oriented correctional boot camp programs as alternatives to incarceration and incapacitation. Many of these initiatives have historically ignored the importance of improving participants' attitudes and employability, while focusing solely on reducing re-offense statistics. The inherent quelling of individualization and lack of intensive treatment are diametrically opposed to the goal of recidivism reduction through rehabilitation (MacKenzie et al., 1995; Stincomb, 1999).

However, this does not outright preclude the possibility that these programs may be salvaged. Rather, policy makers must determine if traditional boot camp programs can be effectively supplemented or otherwise combined with intensive treatment protocols. Unemployment remains one of the most significant predictors of recidivism (Kempinen & Kurylchek, 2003; Nally et al., 2012). Ergo, it is necessary to improve education and vocational rehabilitation programs as well as provide substance abuse counseling if intensive boot camp treatment initiatives are to be effective at reducing recidivism and prison overcrowding by improving the attitudes and employability of graduates.

Though it remains an obscure topic in the literature, the relationship between employability and recidivism is significant. Simply releasing offenders into the communities from which they came and expecting them not to re-offend is tantamount to a coin toss. However, contemporary recidivism data convey that nonviolent offenders, particularly those of younger age demographics, have far greater than a 50/50 chance of rearrest (Nally et al., 2012). Nonetheless, the efficacy of employment intervention through probation agencies has been empirically substantiated. However, previous programs have not been necessarily studious in selecting participants (Hancock & Raeside, 2009). The evidence calls for a paradigm shift in the philosophy of correctional rehabilitation; one which instills discipline without sacrificing individualism and measures success through reintegration rather than through punishment.

Part Two:
Ethics & Public Safety

IV

Ethical Considerations in Criminal Justice Research: Informed Consent and Confidentiality

The use of human subjects has become prevalent in criminal justice research, which presents myriad ethical concerns regarding the civil rights of vulnerable parties. In such studies, researchers maintain considerable, potentially dangerous, influence over participants due to their knowledge and perceived authority. This paradigm was presented in Milgram's classic obedience experiments which affirmed the power of situational forces on human behavior. Consequently, human participants may be unnecessarily subjected to harmful situations due to improper research practices and ethical problems (Juritzen, Grimen, & Heggen, 2011; Mulvey & Phelps, 1988; Reeder, Monroe, & Pryor, 2008).

However, Rhineberger (2006) concluded that discussions of research ethics were virtually absent from introductory criminal justice textbooks. On average, introductory criminology course materials dedicated only one page to ethical issues; none of which were covered in significant detail. This neglect of ethical considerations conveys that these topics are of little importance to criminological research. Ostensibly, these omissions appear to represent indifference among scholars and ethics committees and have exposed researchers to legal ramifications.

Citing a lack of adequate guidance, Bloomberg and Wilkins (1977) conveyed the need for professional societies to implement codes of ethics and corresponding sanctions relevant to human subject studies in criminal justice research. Specifically, the authors proposed standards which aimed to eliminate potential risks to participants through informed consent and confidentiality policies in order to combat the possibility of governmental intervention. Similar ethical codes were eventually adopted by the Academy of Criminal Justice Sciences and the American Society of Criminology. However, these policies have not effectively allayed the potential for conflict regarding evidentiary and testimonial privileges or addressed similar legal threats to confidentiality (Lowman & Palys, 2001). Given the difficulty of implementing comprehensive ethical research practices in the field of criminal justice, codified policies regarding informed consent and confidentiality are necessary to ensure the protection of both researchers and vulnerable subjects.

Historical Context

Most regard the protection from unnecessary risk as a fundamental human right. This precedent was affirmed on an international scale with the post-World War II adoption of the Nuremberg Code, which prohibits reckless and nonconsensual experimentation on human subjects (Kauzlarich & Kramer, 1998, p. 35). Accordingly, research subjects are afforded the discretion to divulge or omit personal information as well as refuse or submit to participation. Moreover, they must be properly informed of potential risks and the implications of consent (Bloomberg & Wilkins, 1977). However, informed consent requirements have historically been ignored by social agencies in experiments involving the use of prisoners and other "undesirables" whom criminal justice scholars routinely study.

During the 1940s, researchers from the United States National Institute of Health deliberately infected over 1,400 Guatemalan prisoners, prostitutes, and mental health patients with various sexually-transmitted diseases in order to assess the effectiveness of penicillin treatment protocols (Reverby, 2011; Semeniuk, 2010). Similarly, over the course of a decade beginning in 1963, 131 convicted offenders under the custody of the Oregon and Washington State prison systems were exploited so that researchers could determine the effects of irradiation on testicular function (Kauzlarich & Kramer, 1998, pp. 132-140). Also during the 1960s, at least three separate psychotherapy research teams in the United States and The Netherlands administered psychedelic compounds such as LSD and psilocybin to inmates in unsuccessful attempts to modify behavior and reduce recidivism (Doblin, 1998).

Researchers have also purportedly conducted experiments on prisoners which involved simulated explosive burns, the injection of live cancer cells, electric shock therapies, and even castration. Though acts of fraud, assault, and murder are generally punished in accordance with the law, researchers who have engaged in these activities in the course of scientific inquiry have historically evaded sanction, largely due to their comparably heightened social status. While such extreme examples of disreputable medical studies are no longer common, due to subsequent government intervention in the 1970s, they serve as a reminder of the need for ethics policies and have revealed a general disregard for the rights of vulnerable research participants who have been stigmatized by the justice system. Nevertheless, the federal government recently considered revising the regulations which govern the use of prisoners as experimental subjects so as to make offenders more accessible to researchers (Richardson, 2009; Waltz, 2006).

Informed Consent

In order to legitimately obtain consent, researchers must provide subjects with an explanation of the experimental process; describe the discomforts, risks, and expected benefits; disclose advantageous alternative procedures; offer answers to procedural questions; and inform participants that they are free to withdraw from the study at will (Bloomberg & Wilkins, 1977). Most importantly, research participants must possess a demonstrable capacity to decide and submit voluntarily. Therefore, informed consent constitutes the delivery of this information to all research subjects so that they may knowingly and legally consent to participation in research studies free from duress, deception, or coercion (Erlen, 2010; O'Neill, 2003).

However, controversy has surrounded the modern informed consent doctrine which began in 1957 with the California Court of Appeals decision in *Salgo v. Leland Stanford Jr. University Board of Trustees* and its detrimental impact on the fiduciary researcher-subject relationship (Berry, 2005). Criminal justice scholars are left to discern whether or not their subjects, some under custodial supervision, are able to legitimately volunteer themselves. Ensuring true comprehension and voluntary participation becomes even more laborious when research enters into different cultural settings, such as in state-crime studies of developing nations (Bhutta, 2004).

Ethical considerations regarding informed consent in criminal justice research are unique as punishment and treatment are often inextricably linked. Consequently, research participants may have already been labeled by the justice system and find it difficult to accept the objectivity and purported benefits of experimentation; which may compel them to withhold potentially damaging information. This trend is particularly pronounced in juvenile justice research.

Moreover, subjects may be unable to provide legitimate consent due to potential coercion. Thereby, refusal to consent may negatively impact participants' willingness to accept treatment as perceived by authority figures. Contrarily, subjects may misrepresent themselves during the course of a particular study in an attempt to improve their image in the eyes of justice administrators. This conflict is further exacerbated by the lack of definitive outcome assessments, which makes it difficult for researchers to present a realistic appraisal of risks and benefits (Mulvey & Phelps, 1988). Such ambiguity can expose researchers to legal repercussions for failure to provide full disclosure.

Confidentiality

Criminal justice research often requires respondents to disclose information relevant to criminal and subversive activity, some of which may remain unknown to authorities. Therefore, researchers are ethically obligated to protect their data so that it may not be used against participants in legal proceedings. If no such guarantee can be given, a study may be corrupted as vulnerable subjects refuse to disclose damaging information. Ergo, confidentiality is vital to ensuring the accuracy of criminological study. According to the respective ethics codes of the American Sociological Association and American Society of Criminology, confidential information provided by research participants must be protected by researchers even in the event that the information is not expressly governed by legal doctrine.

However, no legal protections are described which may benefit researchers in their refusal to breach confidentiality agreements. From a purely ethical standpoint, researchers should only breach confidentiality if the subject specifically consents to the breach, the information is already in the public domain, and/or public interest in disclosure outweighs the interest in maintaining confidence. However, criminal justice researchers may be exposed to three different types of legal conflict concerning research ethics: the obligation to report certain crimes as prescribed in mandatory reporting laws; learning of potential or intended future crimes that may harm third parties; and being subpoenaed to testify in court on issues pertaining to a particular research participant or crime. Beginning with an attempted third-party subpoena of the Kinsey Institute at Indiana University, the secondary legal literature which has developed since the 1970s, particularly out of the civil litigation discovery process, has severely threatened research confidentiality (Bond, 1992; Lowman & Palys, 2001). Consequently, criminal justice researchers have historically resisted requests for confidential research information on ethical grounds, oftentimes without any legal protection.

Confidentiality concerns are even more complex in studies of juvenile offenders. The American juvenile justice system has focused primarily on accountability, recompense, and public safety concerns to the detriment of rehabilitation and research confidence. In the majority of states, juvenile proceedings are open to the public and media, while records are readily disclosed to other public agencies (Webb, 2008). As minor research subjects are not legally autonomous, family and community interests must be factored into the development of confidentiality contracts. While communities may be legitimately concerned with the development of responsible citizens, families are afforded privacy protection in decisions to raise their children free from unnecessary intrusion. Accordingly, researchers must acknowledge these potentially conflicting interests when presented with confidentiality issues. Therefore, scholars in this area of study are sometimes forced to reveal confidential information in the event that it threatens a third party, but must always consider the potential harm that disclosure may have on the juvenile (Mulvey & Phelps, 1988).

Conclusion

Societal perceptions of marginalized groups have contributed to historical instances of unethical experimentation on vulnerable participants, prompting significant governmental intervention. Subjects are now afforded protection through informed consent requirements, though the potential for coercion has not been eliminated. Moreover, contemporary laws present ethical dilemmas which may force researchers to violate the trust of those who provide self-deprecating information for the purposes of criminological inquiry. Nonetheless, the validity of criminal justice research hinges upon the protection of stigmatized individuals and confidential information. Professional societies have since adopted codes of ethics in order to safeguard the civil rights of research subjects. However, researchers remain exposed to legal ramifications regarding the refusal to breach confidentiality agreements for the benefit of third parties.

V

Cause and Effect of Police Excessive Force

American peace officers are granted the authority to utilize non-lethal and lethal force in specific circumstances in accordance with their training. Therein, the officer unremittingly assesses the situation and incorporates his or her training and judgment in order to determine the most practical response option relative to the prescribed use of force continuum. This delicate process requires the officer to think critically while making sudden, albeit potentially life-altering decisions. Notably, the nature of police work in itself may cloud the necessarily impartial judgment of individual officers as implied by angry aggression theory. The outcome of such encounters relies primarily on the individual officer's ability to perceive and recognize actual threats and to react accordingly.

Ultimately, a use of force incident is scrutinized by law enforcement administrators and the public; and oftentimes the media as well as legislators of criminal and/or civil law. Occasionally, it is consequently determined that the level of force used exceeds the accepted notion of the level justified under the circumstances. Such use is often referred to as excessive force. Certain publicized excessive force incidents, current use of force policies, and the implementation of zero-tolerance and/or legalistic-style enforcement in some jurisdictions have conjured public concern regarding police use of force. Whether the force is the action of an individual officer or reveals an apparent policy within the agency itself, these incidents prompt a perusal of the officer and his or her department by the public and media (U.S. Department of Justice, 1999). It should be the goal of police administrators to ensure that public opinion agrees that the department and its officers truly exist to protect and serve their respective communities. Proper use of force policies must be implemented with this notion in mind.

Psychological Factors and Causes of Aggressive Police Behavior

To solely analyze the effectual consequences of excessive force would not precipitate a comprehensive understanding of the issue. As profound as such force incidents are with respect to community relations and inter-departmental turmoil, identifying the root causes of aggressive behavior may shed light into the cavern of aggressive tendencies which prompt the use of excessive force. Griffin and Bernard (2003) argued that the chronic stress and social isolation inherent to police work not only increase an officer's perception of threats and aggressiveness of response, but effectively raise his or her tendency to utilize aggression on visible and vulnerable targets. Herein, we can ascertain that the very act of preserving the peace subjects officers to an environment wherein their own behavior is altered and gravitates toward the use of disproportional force responses.

There are three primary psychological factors which influence aggressive behavior in police officers according this theory. First, officers endure chronic arousal due to on-the-job stressors. Threats to an officer's well-being are omnipresent in the mind as rightfully they should be. Though life-threatening encounters with citizens and criminals may be infrequent, they continually loom in the officer's subconscious. Actual encounters and the accompanying thoughts are compounded in effectiveness by the presence of bulletins and briefs wherein the officer is educated and reminded of the latest weaponry which is to be used against him/her and the reiteration of past events which have claimed the lives of fellow officers.

Secondly, the inability of the officer to actually respond to the direct cause or causes of this stress only compounds its impact. The individual officer can do little, if anything, to remedy the effects of stressors such as implied danger, media relations, citizen hostility and political pressure. Accordingly, the stress continues to mound while alleviation is difficult to achieve. In fact, merely attempting to respond to these stressors may only further agitate the officer.

Lastly, social isolation may influence an officer both at work and in his or her personal life. Most researchers agree that this isolation is mostly self-imposed. Ultimately, officers may become distrustful of others, particularly the conventional citizens who they are actually policing, but also their command staff and superiors within their own organization. Additionally, there is little an officer can do to leave this isolation behind when not in uniform. Neighbors, friends, and relatives tend to identify them as policemen whether on duty or not. Separately, each of these factors place officers in a unique position during their day-to-day life. However, their combined effect leaves individual officers vulnerable to developing an undesirable psychological disposition.

Inarguably, police officers are encumbered by chronic stress of which there is little hope of escape and a plethora of literature supports the notion that they are socially isolated both on the job and in their personal lives. Angry aggression theory proposes that people who endure chronic psychological arousal tend to see threats more frequently and respond to threats more aggressively than most others. Moreover, when chronically aroused people become socially isolated, the aforementioned perceptions and responses become embedded into the individual's accepted norms and worldview. Ultimately, if such a person is unable to respond to the source of the stress, he or she will likely convey aggression onto readily accessible visible and vulnerable targets (Griffin & Bernard, 2003). This hypothesis offers an explanation as to why police officers perceive threats more frequently and respond more aggressively than most others would deem appropriate. Moreover, it substantiates the reasoning behind the existence of the police subculture and the accepted norms which comprise its worldview. Tendencies toward disproportional force response and excessive force incidents may very well be the product of day-to-day peace-keeping operations.

The Role of Technology in Police Use of Force Training

Modern police use of force training generally incorporates an illustrated "Use of Force Continuum." Such models are designed to aid police officers in determining which level of force is appropriate in response to a given resistance level in any situation. According to Michael E. Miller (2010), an effective continuum should be arranged into six categories of escalating suspect resistance and the proportional corresponding officer's use of force: (1) No resistance: Officer presence; (2) Verbal noncompliance: Verbal commands; (3) Passive resistance: Hands-on tactics, chemical spray; (4) Active resistance: Intermediate weapons such as baton, Taser, strikes, non-deadly force; (5) Aggressive resistance: Intermediate weapons with intensified force, non-deadly force; (6) Deadly-force resistance: Deadly force.

The aforementioned continuum is not a comprehensively accepted model. However, it serves as a general guide for police administrators to incorporate into the policies of their respective departments. Citizens should appreciate how the advent of non-lethal controls has diversified the officer's "toolbox" in recent decades. Modern police officers receive comparatively superior training regarding hands-on tactics as well as chemical sprays and Tasers in an effort to reduce suspect deaths and officer injuries.

Currently, debate among law enforcement agencies ensues over where electronic control devices (i.e. Tasers) should be placed in the continuum. Initially, numerous police administrators chose to permit the usage of electronic control weapons in response to passive resistance; defined as the suspect's failure to obey verbal direction with no direct threat of officer injury. Subsequently, use of force incidents resulting from such ill-advised policies regarding Taser employment in decidedly low-intensity situations prompted considerable media attention and public controversy (Miller, 2010).

Primarily, opponents of lax Taser regulations cite that officers on average seem to employ electronic control devices far too liberally and in situations wherein hands-on tactics or Oleoresin Capsicum (OC) Spray would suffice. In light of the fact that, unlike MK-4 OC Spray and other non-lethal controls, Tasers have been responsible for a considerable numbers of deaths in America, numerous civil rights groups have publicly expressed outrage with regard to the lack of regulation on police Taser use. In the globalized world of readily-accessible media outlets, the unjustified death of even one individual at the hands of police can reach the eyes and ears of millions of concerned citizens almost instantaneously. It is often at this exact moment that most citizens conveniently repress any fond memories they may have harbored toward police officers and replace them with newsreel footage.

The American Civil Liberties Union (ACLU) noted that Tasers were responsible for the deaths of 148 people in the United States and Canada between 1999 and 2005. However, a survey of police departments in central and northern California revealed that such electronic control devices were widely unregulated. Notably, the survey also revealed that only 4 of the 50 departments actually restricted the number of times that an officer may fire a Taser at an individual suspect. This is particularly alarming as Andrew Washington of Vallejo, California died after being Tasered 17 times in a span of only three minutes (ACLU, 2005).

Many agencies have since decided to increase the required level of resistance for Taser employment from passive to active; defined as actions which constitute a suspect's intent to escape or evade arrest without likelihood of officer injury. Unfortunately, Michael E. Miller (2010) noted that this step alone may not necessarily prove to be a viable remedy for decreasing suspect deaths or preventing officer injuries as it is not yet substantiated by independent research. Herein, we gain some perspective into the necessity for law enforcement administrators to recognize that policy changes may have far-reaching effects on public opinion and to act accordingly if an amicable relationship is to be fostered and maintained.

Legal Safeguards against Excessive Force

Conventional citizens would likely agree that excessive police force is intolerable and has no place in a free and democratic society. Nonetheless, problems persist and new incidents arise on occasion to remind us that no man or woman can be wholly trusted with authority if individual rights are to be preserved. Such is why we advocate the principles of law and due process. Specific to police use of excessive force, legislators have seen fit to implement laws not only to reprimand misfeasor officers, but also to adjudicate those officers who sit idly by and allow such an incident to transpire. Various federal criminal and civil laws, as well as state tort laws, may be introduced as a means of reprimand thereafter.

In some instances shy of brutality, an officer may not necessarily be charged under criminal law. Most commonly, such suits cite the Civil Rights Act, Title 42 United States Code section 1983. Notably, certain suits may not be viable under the Civil Rights Act or other federal laws. However, tort laws are very specific in this regard and will likely prompt a civil suit against the misfeasor officer and able officers who neglected to intervene in the matter. According to Benjamin Ferrell (1988), law enforcement officers are permitted the authority to subvert certain civil rights during the performance of their duties. Moreover, they are legally bound to intervene at such a time as a fellow officer betrays the privileges he or she has been granted, lest they be charged alongside the transgressing officer.

It is important to note that failure to intervene in an excessive force incident precipitated by a fellow officer is not charged under respondent superior doctrine. Rather, the nonfeasor officer in such an instance is regarded as a direct participant in the act. Herein, we are also reminded that simply because an act may be technically legal with regard to criminal law, civil sanctions may be introduced as a means of punishment. A person may even be adjudged as innocent in criminal court only to later be found liable for the same offense in civil court. Whether or not the case is tried in criminal court, it is not uncommon for civil suits against the misfeasor officer, present officers, and/or the police department itself to follow.

Perceptions of Police Misconduct

Oftentimes, reality is determined by individual or sub-cultural perception. Generally, public opinion regarding police misconduct flows with the ebb of media coverage and contemporary issues. Historically, law enforcement agencies were notoriously corrupt and discriminatory by modern standards; a fact which has loomed over the heads of police administrators ever since and has proven difficult to remedy. Perhaps peaking during the American civil rights movement, public perception regarding police misconduct and practices continues to oppose the professional image which many departments have invested decades to develop. Primarily, the presence of negative public opinion has been precipitated by media coverage of police brutality (Son & Rome, 2004). Today, the presence of personal video equipment and accessibility to the Internet guarantees that misfeasor officers run a high risk of being caught in the act.

According to Son and Rome (2004), arguably the most prevalent event in recent American history which demonstrated police misconduct to the nation was the 1991 Rodney King beating in Los Angeles, California. Almost a perfect incarnation of police brutality and racism, an amateur cameraman captured a video recording of several White officers beating Mr. King, an African-American. The video was widely spread and went viral across the country via media outlets. As seeing is believing, Americans of all nationalities glimpsed perhaps their first enactment of police brutality, which up until that point was merely an intangible social concern in most minds; particularly those of White Americans.

A Gallup Poll taken after the incident revealed that 68 percent of respondents believed that similar incidents occurred rather frequently. During the ensuing nationwide sense of heightened awareness of the subject, several other police departments were berated with serious misconduct charges to include drug trafficking, unjustified shootings, receipt of bribes, and the sale of confidential information. While such incidents may have gone previously unnoticed, public awareness and outrage ensured that such misconduct was brought to light.

Police administrators contend that such acts are committed by a comparably small number of "bad apple" officers. The evidence appears to support this assertion as very few officers are ever actually convicted on misconduct charges. Regardless, this fact only exacerbates the public perception that incidents continue to occur quite frequently, albeit free from the application of justice. Notably, such polls merely reflect personal beliefs and do not necessarily illustrate life experiences of factual data. Nonetheless, public perception and relations do not rest on factual evidence and are often determined solely by the beliefs and opinion of the populace. Regardless of the infrequency of police brutality incidents, the public continues to believe that such incidents are commonplace and demands adjudication of the officers. The citizenry requires a comfortable feeling that such behavior is not tolerated by authority figures or elected officials and will be responded to with adequate legal measures to satisfy their penchant for justice.

Conclusion

The nature of a police-citizen encounter requiring the application of the use of force continuum is a delicate process wherein the officer bears the burden of responding within proportional and appropriate measures. Notably, multiple psychological factors inherent to the pursuance of police duties may effectively and unnecessarily increase aggressive tendencies and disproportionate responses among officers. Given this penchant, officers may utilize the most forceful means available to them as their perception of the level of actual danger may be convoluted. Furthermore, it is necessary for police administrators to recognize that the implementation of non-lethal control devices must be categorically aligned within the force continuum.

Failure to do so prompts the lenient and ample use of these measures by police officers wherein non-forceful means may be available and offers no punishment under departmental regulations by which to reprimand officers. Recent history has been wrought with the introduction of numerous civil rights and tort laws aimed at limiting misconduct and discriminatory practices which are a product of improper police policy and management. Subsequently, public opinion continues to recognize police departments by considering the worst police brutality incidents in their memory. It is the responsibility of administrators to convey a renovation of the old policing methods and regain public favor.

VI

Effects of the "Blue Wall of Silence" on Officer and Organizational Integrity

An integrity system is a compendium of institutional guidelines and procedures which encourage compliance with minimum ethical standards and the pursuit of ethical ideals from organizational members. Since the integrity of any professional or quasi-professional group is largely dependent upon the moral behavior of its members, occupational integrity systems aim to develop individual compliance with moral principles. Importantly, the moral principles which govern action are relatively dependent upon the type of occupation (Miller, 2010). For example, while deception may be regarded as unethical in financial transactions, police officers are expected to deceive suspects during interrogation within legally and organizationally defined limits.

Organizations which cannot equitably manage these moral conflicts often nurture environments which are conducive to employee misconduct (Wolfe & Piquero, 2011). Also, the relative association between morality and occupation demands that those who choose to undertake a particular profession, such as police work, must develop a specific moral character in order to meet their professional obligations. Most importantly, these occupationally specific moral obligations are utilized in order to assess an officer's ability to discharge his or her duties (Miller, 2010).

The integrity of a police organization relies on three basic components; structure, function, and culture. Structurally, a department must maintain legal and administrative processes relative to promotions, citizen complaints, and discipline, as well as promote fairness, procedural justice, and transparency. Functionally, law enforcement agencies must implement organizational procedures which align with their legitimate functions; such as equitable justice and the protection of individual human rights. The organizational ethos, or culture, should encourage exceptional performance and be intolerant of both incompetence and misconduct. However, cultures vary dramatically between occupational fields (Miller, 2010). Ergo, loyalty is often a tenant of the police culture given the dangerous masculine nature of the work and need for solidarity (Gottschalk, 2011). Consequently, this loyalty lays the foundation upon which rests the "blue wall of silence."

Challenges Posed by the Blue Wall

According to Gottschalk (2011), the blue wall (a.k.a. code of silence or blue curtain) is an informal prohibition against reporting the misconduct of fellow officers within the police culture. Thereby, it defends unethical practices such as the acceptance of gratuities and the use of excessive force while weakening deterrence measures aimed at reducing corruption. Generally, police officers are honorable and competent public servants. However, when serious incidents of misconduct occur within law enforcement agencies, there is a tendency to blame mismanagement, ambiguous procedural guidelines, and lack of resources rather than view them as individual criminal acts. Accordingly, the code of silence protects disreputable officers from organizations perceived to be unjust and incompetent; ostensibly defending the "bad apples" from the situational influence of a "bad barrel."

According to Shockley-Eckles (2011), the "officer shuffle" is but one of the undesirable byproducts of the blue wall. Therein, discredited officers are simply transferred between departments so that they may remain within the police culture free from significant repercussions, even though 43 states currently mandate the revocation of the state license of any officer found to have engaged in misconduct. However, these officers are commonly permitted to resign and often conduct lateral moves to other unsuspecting law enforcement agencies. Though this is one example of how the blue wall protects unethical officers and saves departments from public embarrassment, those who eventually work alongside such transferred cops find it difficult to maintain their allegiance to the unwritten code of silence.

Implementing Controls

Rothwell and Baldwin (2007) investigated nine policy and procedural variables as predictors of officers' willingness to "blow the whistle" on seven forms of police misconduct. They affirmed that officers are actually more likely to report major (felony) violations, though are less likely to report minor (misdemeanor) violations, than are civilian public service employees within their respective agencies. This may indicate that police officers are more likely to engage in noble cause justifications when presented with minor conduct violations. Most importantly, the study revealed that the presence of a departmental mandatory reporting policy and supervisory status of the officer were significantly and positively related to an individual officer's willingness to report incidents of misconduct. Moreover, only supervisory status was found to be significantly related to the frequency of reporting minor violations.

The most conspicuous implication of this research is that the "blue wall of silence" may not be as formidable as previously believed. Indeed, Lamboo (2010) affirmed that as many as two-thirds of internal investigations are the result of internal reports from police officers. The need to identify and recognize ethical officers for selection and promotion is axiomatic, due to the observed association between supervisory status and both willingness to report and frequency of reporting. For instance, police organizations, particularly those with fewer sworn officers, may benefit from the adoption of a combination general mental ability-integrity test during the recruit selection process (Rothwell & Baldwin, 2007). Accordingly, the appointment of ethical supervisors and managers is absolutely vital to combating the negative effects of the blue wall. Officers are less likely to adhere to the code of silence or submit to noble cause justifications of misconduct if they perceive their departments to be fair and just in managerial practices (Wolfe & Piquero, 2011).

Moreover, while mandatory reporting policies increased officers' willingness to report, they did not influence measures of reporting frequency, which indicates that the potential repercussions of reporting, such as being ostracized by the group, may mediate the actual practice of whistle-blowing. Nonetheless, police supervisors are required to enforce policy and report violations. Therefore, ethical supervisors can rely on mandatory reporting policies to support their decisions to blow the whistle and hold fellow officers accountable. Rewarding ethical officers with supervisory positions and backing them with mandatory reporting policies would increase both the willingness to report and legitimate whistle-blowing behavior (Rothwell & Baldwin, 2007).

Part Three:
Psychological & Sociological Considerations

VII

Motivations and Behavioral Characteristics of Serial Arsonists

According to Davis and Lauber (1999), arson is differentiated from fire setting by the malicious intent of the arsonist. Arsonists may receive a material benefit from deliberate fire setting, most commonly by way of insurance funds. Additionally, arson may be utilized as a method for destroying evidence of another crime. These are most often singular offenses with a tangible payoff for the offender. Contrarily, pyromania is an impulse control disorder wherein the pyromaniac suffers from a compulsion to set fires often without the prospect for material gain or an axiomatic motivation. Researchers continue to debate the prevalence of pyromania in arson, though estimates range from extremely rare to as much as 40% of all arson cases (pp. 274). Still other arsonists receive sexual gratification from the act of fire setting, as many serial killers do from the act of murder.

Douglas and Olshaker (1999) affirmed that three youthful behaviors of developing antisocial offenders comprise the homicidal triad; enuresis (bed-wetting), cruelty to animals or small children, and fire starting. These three components were derived from various prison interviews with convicted serial killers and arsonists. Accordingly, the authors assert that the motivation for serial arsonists correlates with that of serial murderers. In fact, serial arson may be a harbinger of a future ascension into more violent crimes such as rape and murder as the offender seeks sexual gratification. For example, David Berkowitz, a.k.a. Son of Sam a.k.a the .44 Caliber Killer, set more than 2,000 fires in the New York City area before graduating into serial murder. Other offenders, like Berkowitz, also confessed to engaging in masturbation while observing their fires, occasionally among the crowd of spectators, which substantiated sexual gratification as a motivation for serial arson. Similar to overtly sexual crimes, arson is often an attempt to gain control and satisfy a need for success in the offender's life. Thereby, the arsonist seeks to manipulate victims, first responders, authority figures, the media, and the community as a whole during the commission of his crime (p. 47-49).

Common Characteristics of Deliberate Fire Setters

In order to understand motive, it is necessary to understand the unique attributes of particular types of offenders. As noted by Davis and Lauber (1999), there is no typified arsonist. However, arsonists exhibit characteristics similar to those of sexual predators and other serial offenders. Though arson is not wholly reserved to a particular gender, the vast majority of arsonists are males. Motives for female arsonists are most often comparably more dramatic than those of their male counterparts. Cases of revenge fire setting or the destruction of a property with a sentimental or symbolic tie to the offender is more commonly associated with the comparably rare crimes of female arsonists. Additionally, multiple arson offenses are decidedly unusual for female offenders. As with other violent serial crimes, serial arson is almost always committed by males.

Generally, arsonists are Caucasian men in their mid to late 20s or early 30s. Most often, they are raised in unstable homes among a large family from lower socioeconomic status. One or both of the parents, at least one of which is often domineering or rejecting, is absent and parental abuse is evident in the childhood of 63% of arsonists. Most possess extensive criminal histories, below average intelligence, and resultant low academic achievement. They are often loners who lack the necessary social skills to foster positive interpersonal and romantic relationships. Male arsonists are generally either unmarried or in an unhealthy relationship and harbor resentment or hatred toward women. Ergo, arson may be utilized as a sexual substitute as a means to compensate for a lack of healthy intimacy.

Arsonists are usually unemployed or in unskilled professions, drifting from job to job due to difficulties with peers and authority figures. Problems associated with career retention are often exacerbated by alcohol abuse. Subsequently, co-workers, superiors, or the business itself may become targets for arson. Compared to violent sex offenders and murderers, arsonists are much more likely to possess a physical abnormality or deformity, as well as poor dental work. The presence of such physical deformations may explain why arsonists who do not graduate to more violent crimes may be content with remaining in the shadows, forgoing face-to-face encounters, since rape and murder are decidedly personal and intimate crimes. Lastly, arsonists often exhibit outward signs of tension and develop neurotic or psychopathic disorders (pp. 277-278). These symptoms often become more axiomatic immediately prior to the beginning of an arsonist's spree. Thereafter, arsonists will often demonstrate an axiomatic curiosity regarding the crime and may even inquire as to the state of the investigation.   It is not uncommon for arsonists to subsequently collect news articles regarding their crimes and pictures of their fires.

Profiling Serial Arsonists with Excitement Motives

The U.S. Fire Administration (2001) attributed 267,000 annual fires to arson in the United States, resulting in over $1.4 billion in yearly property damage. While the majority of arsonists are primarily motivated by monetary gain or vandalism, the most devious offenders do so for the sheer excitement. Ergo, excitement is the most common motivation for serial arsonists.

According to Kocsis and Cooksey (2002), those arsonists seeking excitement set fires as a means to satisfy a deluded heroic desire, sexual fetish, or are living out a psychotic delusion. Regardless of motive, serial arsonists demonstrate common behaviors in the commission of their crimes. The authors noted that the archaic ideal of an organized-disorganized dichotomy of arsonists is invalid. Rather, organization and planning is a common behavior of all serial arson offenses. The fact that evidence is left behind at a particular scene is not indicative of a disorganized arsonist. Instead, it is the nature of the crime itself with virtually guarantees that some form of evidence will remain.

Furthermore, a relationship usually exists between the arsonist and the victim, though the correlation may only be evident in the psychological delusion or internal fantasy of the offender. It is vital for investigators to carefully consider the target as it will provide insight into the identity and/or motive of the offender. Additionally, it is not uncommon for arsonists to enter the target building and steal particular items if available before the fire is set, usually from a single point of origin, regardless of security measures or the presence of onlookers. This notion is diametrically opposed to the behaviors often exhibited by murderers and rapists who are generally deterred by an increased risk of apprehension, which makes the serial arsonists a comparably brazen criminal. Given these data, the authors asserted that serial arson is not often a crime of opportunity committed against a susceptible target. Rather, the arsonist most often chooses a particular victim or target in accordance with his own deluded fantasy; i.e. a particular business, industry, or type of person (pp. 646-647).

While psychologists commonly study an individual in order to predict behavior, successful profilers must analyze behavior (i.e. the crime) and reverse the process in order to profile the type of individual who is responsible. Arsonists exhibiting the sexual pattern associate the act of fire setting with sexual excitement and gratification. The most distinguishing behavior therein is the commission of sexual activity at or near the crime scene. Such offenders often remain at the scene and during the extinguishments. Sexually-motivated arsons are most often committed on week days during autumn and winter.

The wanton arsonist pattern is characterized by a general animosity toward a vague class of targets, such as schools, commercial properties, or business establishments. Therein, the arsonist will commonly ignite a particular item or items within the targets, which holds some specific meaning to the offender. However, instances wherein targets appear sporadic or unrelated do not necessarily denote an unsophisticated offender. Therein, the motive may simply be pure thrill. It is not uncommon for thrill-seeking arsonists to engage in seemingly sporadic fire setting in order to practice their art and develop more cogent methods for creating more dramatic fires.

Thrill-seeking arsonists are often comparably older and have more steady employment than most arsonists. Both wanton and thrill arsonists generally engage in fire setting on weekends during the spring and summer (Kocsis & Cooksey, 2002, pp. 646-650). By studying the target, origin of the fire, and the crowd of onlookers, investigators can determine which behavioral pattern was most closely exhibited by the arsonist in order to build an accurate profile.

VIII

Learning Disabilities as Harbingers of Delinquency

In recent decades, various diagnoses of behavioral disorders have become common among American youths; the most common being attention deficit disorder (ADD) and attention deficit hyperactivity disorder (ADHD). According to Miller (2008), the first mainstream childhood behavioral disorder, Minimal Brain Dysfunction, was diagnosed by psychiatrists in the late 1960s. Minimal Brain Dysfunction entails mild to severe learning or behavioral disabilities indicative of improper functioning of the central nervous system and is presently diagnosed in correlation or interchangeably with ADD and/or ADHD.

By 2008, over six million American children aged 5 to 19 years old were receiving antipsychotic or psychotropic medication to curb the symptoms of ADD or ADHD. A study of schoolchildren in Atlanta, Georgia revealed that roughly one-third were diagnosed with a learning or behavioral disorder. Given the prevalence of these disorders, their effect on antisocial and deviant personality development is of great concern to criminologists and mental health professionals.

Robins and Rutter (1990) noted that common learning disabilities are characterized by developmentally inappropriate degrees of inattention, impulsivity, and/or hyperactivity. Inattention is evident in activities such as transitioning from one incomplete task onto another and has obvious implications for substandard academic achievement. Impulsivity implies messy or careless work habits, as well as failure to heed instruction and an inclination to engage in dangerous activity without consideration of potentially negative outcomes, hindering the development of reasoning abilities. Disorders incorporating hyperactivity include the added symptom of excessive restlessness and fidgeting, most commonly prevalent in children and adolescents.

The aforementioned traits, especially impulsivity, demonstrate a potential for future antisocial personality disorders and deviant behavior. It is also noteworthy that child hyperactivity and inattention can predict low subsequent academic achievement, which is known to be a factor in the development of delinquent tendency (p. 62-64). While an ADHD diagnoses does not denote an inherent penchant for criminality, the compendium of symptoms convey a risk for deviance and misconduct if not brought under control.

The co-morbidity of ADHD and environmental risk factors yields evidence of the correlation between learning disorders and deviance. Moreover, these symptoms and factors complement each other and effectively accelerate the downward spiral into delinquency. Essentially, children with ADHD who display conduct problems mature into adults of similar disposition who thereafter rear their offspring in like fashion. While the direct causation of criminality from ADHD is difficult to quantify due to external factors, a conspicuous relationship has been revealed via behavioral studies of various populations of prison inmates and those diagnosed with paraphilias. The evidence of this association is axiomatic.

ADHD in Childhood and Adolescence

Controversy among professionals and scholars persists as to whether ADHD in children is a precursor to deviance or a product of other risk factors and environmental processes. Regardless, its quantitative association with misconduct is undeniable. According to Savolainen et al. (2010), various studies have concluded that convicted offenders meet the criteria for ADHD diagnosis at a rate of approximately 45-50%. Unfortunately, the existence of additional risk factors and environmental processes, such as family adversity and educational failure, has hindered scientific analysis into the relationship between ADHD and deviant behavior. Therefore, it is difficult to identify whether ADHD is a cause or an effect of criminal tendencies. However, most researchers agree that this link demands further inquiry since these factors appear to be mutually supportive (p. 443).

Savolainen et al. (2010) opposed the notion that a diagnosis of ADHD is inherently indicative of future criminality. Nonetheless, the authors proposed that it is to be regarded as a risk factor to the extent that it inhibits the formulation of strong social bonds in accordance with social control theory. Notably, children diagnosed with ADHD have difficulty forging strong ties to parents, peers, and conventional institutions due to hyperactivity and inattention. Ultimately, ADHD symptoms have a negative correlation with educational attainment and aspirations, which contribute to a lower socioeconomic position in adult life. This is often due to frustration and a fatalistic misconception that learning is an exercise in futility. The lack of strong social bonds is further exacerbated by poor interpersonal skills, which are generally evident in the parents of ADHD children as well. Consequently, children with ADHD are often shunned by conventional peers and thereby forced to associate with delinquents since conventional middle-class goals become ever-increasingly distant (p. 445-446). Having severed, or never having established, ties with conventional expectation, these individuals gravitate toward deviant peer groups.

Savolainen et al. (2010) noted that "adolescent symptoms of ADHD have a substantial casual effect on criminal activity" (p. 452). In fact, the risk of future felony conviction for someone with ADHD symptoms was three times higher than that of a person without. This data was particularly influenced by a lack of verbal ability (verbal deficit) which emerged as the most significant predictor of criminal behavior (p. 451-453). Verbal deficits are resultant of ADHD symptoms as inattention and hyperactivity hinder educational attainment and learning capabilities. Subsequently, children with ADHD who fail to formulate adequate social bonds and educational aspirations are predisposed to misconduct and criminality. Notably, further research is required to substantiate the causational relation that ADHD has on verbal deficits and vice versa. ADHD is validated as a risk factor for misconduct, though separating various environmental processes and factors precludes evidence of direct causation.

Adult ADHD and the Family

Children with ADHD will, if their symptoms are not controlled or treated, inevitably mature into adults who suffer from behavioral or personality disorders. Muslow, O'Neal, and McBride (2001) noted that 30-50% of children diagnosed with ADHD continue to exhibit inattention and impulsivity well into adulthood, though hyperactivity seems to wane. Consequently, the authors affirmed that only 1% to 5% of adults display symptoms diagnosable as ADHD. It is common for these adults to rear children who suffer from ADHD as well. ADHD remains "one of the most genetically linked of all psychological disorders" (pp. 39).

ADHD in a family setting often contributes to increased stress and limited coping methods which hinder effective child rearing. The behavioral byproducts of ADHD can prompt child maltreatment and effectively arrest the social and psychological development of exposed children. ADHD is regarded as a risk factor for child maltreatment due to its known correlation with behavioral and personality maladjustments. Potential products of ADHD include "substance abuse, depression, impulsivity, isolation, unemployment, low educational attainment, unintended pregnancy, and relationship disruption" (p. 36). In accordance with social learning theory, children learn deviant and criminal behaviors via the same cognitive methods as any other convention. Thus, tendencies toward impropriety may be implanted in children as a result of association with family members who suffer from ADHD. Thereafter, as these children mature, the cycle continues through their own children and family members.

Obviously, substance abuse and impulsivity significantly reduce one's likelihood of becoming a productive member of a cohesive society since clouded judgment and unpredictable behavior promote instability. Likewise, unemployment, low educational attainment, and unintended pregnancies (particularly at an early age) can confine an individual into a lower socio-economic status for a lifetime and place aspirations and gratification further out of reach. Such a disposition may prompt underprivileged individuals to engage in criminal activity as a means to expedite gratification. Therein, conventional middle-class expectations become increasingly foreign to them. Depression and isolation may appear at face value to be individual plights with little interpersonal consequence.

However, according to Muslow, O'Neal, and McBride (2001), family stress theory regards social support as the primary resource for families dealing with particular stressors. Indeed, it is absolutely vital to the maintenance of family cohesion in the face of even every-day stress. Isolation and depression remove the desire for external social support and subsequently arouse families into instability and eventual crisis. Often, this instability prompts child maltreatment which further reduces a child's chances of removing him/herself from the maelstrom (p. 37-38).

Prevalence of ADHD in Prison Inmates

While research has not effectively concluded that ADHD, in and of itself, directly predisposes an individual to criminality, the sheer volume of ADHD-afflicted prison inmates in staggering. Indeed, researchers on both sides of the argument note that the statistics regarding the prevalence of ADHD symptoms within prison populations demand attention. As alluded to previously, Savolainen et al. (2010) argued against a direct association between ADHD and criminal behavior. Nonetheless, the authors noted the pervasiveness of ADHD symptoms in prisoners. There exists a preponderance of evidence in prison behavioral studies which suggests this correlation.

According to T. Einat and A. Einat (2008), low academic attainment and learning disabilities are regarded as risk factors for criminal behavior and antisocial personality disorders. Persons with ADHD are as much as seven times more likely to develop antisocial personalities and substance abuse problems in their adult lives. The negative corroboration of learning disabilities on reading comprehension and academic achievement place afflicted individuals at risk of future criminality. Subsequently, it is of little surprise that delinquent   populations   demonstrate   an   overrepresentation of learning disabilities. The authors affirmed that previous studies of prison populations have confirmed rates of learning disabilities among inmate populations from 30% to 76% (p. 416-421).

In their independent study of Israeli prison inmates, T. Einat and A. Einat (2008) concluded that nearly 70% of subjects were characterized as learning disabled. Over half of these inmates were diagnosable as having ADHD. Furthermore, they concluded that learning disabilities correlated with low levels of education as well a comparably earlier start to criminal careers (p. 423-425). Notably, the direct effect of ADHD on criminality is somewhat unclear as low academic achievement (dropping out of school at an early age) also contributes to increased risk of criminality. Nonetheless, evidence suggests that learning disabilities also contribute to an individual's odds of leaving school early and beginning a criminal career. This is likely caused by the frustration of children in school with learning disabilities and the failure of school systems to keep these children enrolled.

Researchers have postulated that statistics regarding ADHD and criminality have been clouded by the emergence of a separate condition known as Conduct Disorder (CD). According to Vitelli (1996), CD is a more cogent predictor of adult antisocial and criminal behavior than ADHD. Nonetheless, children with both CD and ADHD demonstrate a higher arrest rate and earlier onset of criminal careers than those with CD alone.

Vitelli's (1996) study of maximum security inmates revealed that a childhood diagnoses of ADHD was as much as eight times more prevalent among adult prisoners than in the general public (p. 264-268). The prevalence of both CD and ADHD among the inmates in this study supports the notion that childhood learning and conduct disorders should be regarded as risk factors for criminal behavior. However, it remains difficult to quantify the precise affect that ADHD alone has on criminality as it is often mediated by environmental factors and co-morbidity with other behavioral disorders.

Westmoreland et al. (2010) asserted that, contrary to common belief, ADHD is a stronger predictor of adult misconduct than CD, regardless of the presence of substance abuse. In accordance with previous research, the authors concluded that the prevalence of ADHD among prison populations exceeded the rate found in the non-offender populous nearly six-fold. Furthermore, they affirmed that in offenders with ADHD, gender differences played no significant role in the development of criminal behavior. It is also evident that offenders with ADHD demonstrate a high probability of having additional personality, mood, and anxiety disorders as well as psychotic disorders, particularly schizophrenia. It is also noteworthy that a history of childhood Conduct Disorder was more than twice as prevalent in individuals with ADHD (p. 362-365).

A preponderance of evidence substantiating the link between learning disabilities and criminal behavior is found in the aforementioned studies. While a plethora of environmental and concurrent risk factors may contribute to criminality, ADHD remains a viable predictor of future deviance and misconduct as the childhood symptoms reverberate throughout adulthood. ADHD is emerging as a primary influence in the development of adult behavioral disorders and delinquency.

ADHD and Paraphilias

It has been demonstrated that ADHD serves to complement various deviant tendencies and personality disorders. However, learning disabilities do not merely promote a general penchant toward deviance, as conveyed by their overrepresentation in offender populations. Rather, ADHD mediates more specific deviant inclinations as well. Paraphilias (PAs) are conditions exemplified by repetitive and "socially deviant sexual arousal" (Kafka and Hennen, 2002, pp. 350). Research indicates that these disorders, non-reliant on concurrent learning disabilities, are often found in offenders with a history of ADHD.

According to Kafka and Hennen (2002), ADHD is the single most common nonsexual condition that quantitatively distinguishes individuals with PAs from other sexually hyperactive persons diagnosed with paraphilia-related disorders (PRDs). In order to appreciate the influence of ADHD, it is important to understand the distinction between PRDs and PAs. PRDs are forms of socially acceptable behaviors such as masturbation and pornography dependence that are persistent and done in excess. Contrarily, PAs cross the boundary into unacceptable and deviant sexual behaviors such as pedophilia, voyeurism, sadism, and/or exhibitionism. Such is why it is vital to understand the variables which may prompt an individual to traverse from PRD into PA behavior (p. 350). The authors determined that over 40% of sex offenders diagnosed with PAs also exhibited symptoms diagnosable as ADHD.

Moreover, when juxtaposed with PRD-diagnosed subjects, participants with PAs were noticeably different as they exhibited a history of low academic achievement, school-related learning/behavioral issues, and substance abuse. Each of the aforementioned factors was cited previously as indicative of ADHD behavior. Notably, these same factors distinguished sex offender paraphiliacs from non-offenders diagnosed with PA or PRD (p. 355). The research suggests that individuals who otherwise may have reserved their actions to a dependence on socially accepted sexual arousal may be prompted to engage in deviant sexual activity due to influences mediated by ADHD.

Conclusion

Persuasive evidence exists which substantiates the association between learning disabilities, particularly ADHD, and criminal behavior. A determination of a direct cause-and-effect relationship therein has thus far remained elusive due to myriad often concurrent environmental influences in test subjects. Nonetheless, the prevalence of ADHD in prison inmate populations, its effect on family cohesiveness, and its influence of paraphilia-related behaviors have been illustrated. Notably, a significant percentage of ADHD symptoms remain prevalent throughout adulthood. Subsequently, sufficient data indicates that childhood learning disabilities can be justly regarded as risk factors for antisocial and criminal behavior.

IX

Why Conformists and the Obedient Reject Moral Rebels

Moral rebels are historically perceived as heroes who hold true to their own principles while others submit themselves to conformity and obedience. Those very few who refuse group influences and dissent, rather than seek acceptance, inspire armchair philosophers and observers to maintain faith in their fellow man. Further, they become a beacon of hope for those who wish to believe that they too would remain true to their own principles amid similar social pressures.

According to Monin, Sawyer, and Marquez (2008), those lone exceptions who stand up against corruption and atrocity are eventually celebrated by the masses as they are contrasted against the indecency of the conformist participants. Consequently, one is compelled to understand why these individuals are so often regarded with contempt by the members of the groups against which they rebel in the name of decency. Most agree on what constitutes acceptable human behavior, yet these rebels are shunned by their peers for their adherence to this unwritten moral code. This paper examines why moral rebels are rejected when their dissent negatively impacts the self-image of the members of the obedient group, as well as how rebels and observers perceive the obedient participants.

Moral rebels and whistleblowers are often resented and even retaliated against by obedient participants. This can sometimes be attributed to the fact that members of the group could potentially suffer consequences due to the rebellion. However, Milgram's obedience paradigm conveyed that retaliation is not always a means of self-preservation employed by the participants. Rather, the conformists in the experiment actually perceived the rebels to be unreliable and inferior. They did not applaud the rebels for their adherence to moral principles, but instead ridiculed them for not staying the course (Monin, Sawyer, Marquez, 2008). Essentially, those directly involved in the activity regarded the rebels' altruism as a selfish, even cowardly, act which placed the experiment in jeopardy. Thereby, they felt that the rebels were unable to make the necessary sacrifices for a greater cause; the experiment.

Reeder, Monroe, and Pryor (2008) concluded that Milgram's obedient participants were relatively indifferent to the suffering produced by their actions. Rather, they focused on appeasing the experimenter(s) and remaining obedient in order to justify their actions. Herein, it is axiomatic that the obedient members chastised those who would refuse to participate for moral reasons based upon the latter's refusal to obey. Accordingly, the obedient participants disregarded individual principles and instead judged others based upon their obedience to the experimenter(s). Such justification is reminiscent of the Nuremberg Trial defendants who were "only following orders." The authors noted that Zimbardo's "bad barrel" polemic was upheld in this regard, as situational cues undoubtedly influenced the Milgram participants. In fact, 65% of these obedient participants endured the entire length of the experiment; ultimately delivering a 450-volt shock to the (confederate) learner.

Reeder, Monroe, and Pryor (2008) also noted that Western perceivers tended to neglect the importance of situational influences. Such is why observers were most often shocked to hear of the results of the Milgram experiment. Generally, the motives, goals, and reasons held by the obedient participants were questioned while the role of the experimenters (situational force) was outright ignored. Thereby, observers made strong overall trait judgments of the conformist participants. Consequently, observers condemned members of the obedient group as a means of psychologically distancing themselves from such "evil" people. Without regard for situational pressures, the only alternative for observers would be to accept that they too were capable of committing such atrocities. Given that Milgram's participants were randomly selected "normal" people, observers employed individual mobility via *dis-identification* in order to facilitate this psychological distancing.

Surprisingly, the actual opinion held by moral rebels of obedient participants held little significance in the rejection process. Contrarily, according to Monin, Sawyer, and Marquez (2008), *imagined rejection,* what the rebel "would have thought," of the obedient group compelled the conformists to reject the moral rebel since they automatically believed that the rebel would have looked down on them for not taking the moral high road. This fear of rejection by the obedient participants prompted them to reject the rebel in order to protect their own moral and adaptive adequacy. Thereby, obedient participants rejected those who rebelled for moral reasons as a means by which to protect their own *self-concepts* because they assumed that the moral rebel would resent them.

Discussion

The above data confirmed that the rejection of moral rebels was primarily influenced by the obedient participants' desire to protect their own self-concepts. According to Smith and Mackie (2007), *social comparison theory* proposes that individuals derive their own self-concepts through comparisons between themselves and others (p.99).   Ergo, conformists disassociated with moral rebels in favor of aligning themselves with similar others; fellow obedient participants.

Notably, the opinions held by moral rebels had no influence on levels of remorse experienced by the obedient group following the close of the experiment. Observers were also found to have employed individual mobility in order to psychologically distance themselves from the obedient participants. It was affirmed that opinions held by observers regarding the moral rebel were primarily influenced by the observers' degree of participation in the experiment; less involvement translated to a higher opinion of the rebel and vice versa. Consequently, these studies supported the *perversity of obedience* hypothesis which proposed that the simple act of obeying during a problematic situation makes individuals like the moral rebel(s) less (Monin, Sawyer, & Marquez, 2008).

Throughout the aforementioned studies, the moral rebels never interacted in any way with either obedient participants or observers.   Rather, participants and observers were only aware of the moral rebels' supposed actions to the extent that those actions were explained by experiment confederates.   While this decreased the likelihood of problematic independent variables influencing the results, real-world scenarios are comparably more complex than those analyzed. These studies focused primarily on imagined rejection and attraction, but were unable to address how direct contact with moral rebels may have affected the data.

Moreover, one is unable to draw a clear conclusion regarding how rebels perceive obedient participants from these data as the rebels in the scenarios were fictitious characters. Additionally, numerous participants' survey results had to be removed from the overall calculations due to their suspicion that the supposedly real scenarios were actually experiments: 10 of 70 participants from Study 1; three of 56 participants from Study 2; and two of 132 participants from Study 3. Given the small participant pools in Studies 1 and 2, it is difficult to accurately quantify the extent to which such suspicion may have spread throughout the group.

The experiment conducted by Monin, Sawyer, and Marquez (2008) analyzed the influence of imagined rejection and attraction among obedient groups and observers in order to study the process by which moral rebels were rejected. In order for this research to be applied to practical situations, further research into the effects of direct interaction with moral rebels by observers and obedient participants is desirable. Moreover, self-reporting should not be utilized as the sole means by which information is gathered from obedient participants as these individuals are likely to withhold information and opinions which may negatively impact their self-concepts if revealed.

X

From Nostalgia to Post-Traumatic Stress Disorder: A Mass Society Theory of Psychological Reactions to Combat

The construct now known as Post-Traumatic Stress Disorder (PTSD) has been a recognized consequence of war for at least as long as historians have been documenting conflicts. Though, the current generation of Operation Enduring Freedom (OEF) and Operation Iraqi Freedom (OIF) veterans does not regard it with as much stigmatization as did those of past wars. For instance, when I was diagnosed with PTSD sometime after my second combat tour, I did not feel as though I was "crazy" or marginalized. Instead, I was relieved to know that the problem had been identified and that the recovery process could begin. However, there is significant difference today in how the disorder is perceived by the military and civilian communities.

Though unknown to most outside of the ranks of professional war-fighters, PTSD has been with man throughout the ages in many forms. Scholars, poets, and playwrights have chronicled its symptoms in some of the world's most ancient writings; to include religious texts, epic poems, and battlefield narratives. First officially identified by Western clinicians in the 17th Century, its moniker has changed repeatedly to reflect public perceptions of the afflicted. The purpose of this paper is to examine how social factors have influenced shifts in civilians' cognitive representations of those who suffer from PTSD and how they have been treated by their government.

PTSD is an example of how personal troubles are inextricably linked to social problems. This very intimate disorder is the byproduct of a collective decision, or at least the initial majority acceptance of such a decision, to send young members of a society to war. Accordingly, Catherall (1986) championed a social healing process intended to be included as part of the treatment regimen for PTSD. She proposed incorporating social interaction treatment in order to expedite the re-assimilation of patients into society.

The archaic Ships of Fools mentality contended that psychologically damaged persons were somehow different and therefore should be excluded from the group (Foucault, 1961/1965, pp. vi-vii). However, this state of affairs says more about the nature of the society than the afflicted. Gradually, mental health professionals have grown to understand that this method is wholly ineffective and serves only to stigmatize. Nevertheless, there are still several social barriers which prevent veterans from seeking treatment for PTSD; not the least of which are uninformed notions of "weakness" and machismo. These beliefs and values interrupt the healing process and further marginalize ailing veterans. Accordingly, it is necessary to investigate the origins and development of these values in order to discern the proper place of veterans suffering from PTSD within contemporary American society.

Mass Society Theory

Mass society theory holds that traditional societies are gradually developing into mass societies, characterized by impersonal social relationship indicative of weakening solidarity (Harper & Leicht, 2011, p. 49). It contends that innovations, particularly technological advances in transport and communications, have brought people together like never before and that the division / specialization of labor have made them more dependent upon one another. However, despite the interdependence, they have grown more estranged as the traditional group ties of family and community are virtually non-existent. Consequently, mores and norms become more flexible and there are few, if any, truly unifying values.

This is undoubtedly especially true in the constitutional democracy of the United States wherein individuality is quite often celebrated. Each individual must assume a multiplicity of roles because there is no fixed concept of status. The resultant confusion causes persons to lose their sense of self and conjures anxiety. A society such as this is tantamount to a cinema theater filled with detached anonymous patrons; individuals detached even from themselves (Bell, 1956). Due to the combination of time spent removed from the rest of society and anxiety-based reactions to combat, veterans may find it particularly difficult to form social bonds under these circumstances.

The terminology used to label psychological reactions to combat has evolved from "nostalgia" and "soldier's heart" to the more impersonal "combat exhaustion" and PTSD. The more recent sobriquets appear to be demonstrably more sterilized and void of humanity (Trimble, 1985). This sort of euphemistic language serves to socially distance observers from the sentient humans who are afflicted with the disorder. The malady becomes perceived as one confined to a select vocation, that of soldier, and therefore solely within the purview of the federal government's ever-expanding duties; which are being increasingly augmented by the efforts of non-profit organizations as people begin to question the competency of their governors.

Any individual or communal responsibility for the treatment of an afflicted veteran appears to be deflected and redirected into the realms of politics and philanthropy. Yellow ribbons and wreaths across America honor an abstract notion of nationalism and sacrifice, not individual troops. The people revere symbols rather than faces and names. Most notably, stopping however briefly to praise these artifacts shields the observer from the guilt associated with inaction. They may praise a martyr, though being confronted with the presence of someone who has returned alive but damaged is often too uncomfortable.

Mass society theory shares a common foundation with the Marxian school of thought. The prevalence of PTSD among veterans is illustrative of an inherent scarcity of resources as explained through the conflict perspective. Incidentally, only a very small percentage of the American population is likely to suffer no negative behavioral symptoms following an armed conflict; sociopaths, psychopaths, and other afflicted persons who are largely discouraged from entering into military service in the first instance. Importantly, this is due to the fact that characteristics such as psychopathy can be viewed as an evolved life strategy from a socio-biological standpoint. Therefore, the percentage of such individuals within any given society must remain below a certain threshold, lest group cohesion completely deteriorate (Mokros et al., 2008).

However, American society still regards war as often necessary, even though human beings share an otherwise useful and natural revulsion against harming members of their own species (Hamblen, 2009). Since it would appear that the majority of soldiers enter into war mostly sane, the issue then becomes a question of recompense and access to treatment. As is most anything of value, these resources are also scarce; hence there has been an historic apprehension by the military and federal government to accept PTSD as a legitimate byproduct of war and offer care to veterans.

For the most part, a different crop of soldiers fights in each new war, each war is perceived and justified differently by the public, and veterans of previous conflicts generally do not strictly align themselves with those currently fighting. For example, many veterans' groups distinguish themselves based upon campaign or whether or not a member actually experienced combat. The veteran demographic is therefore one of myriad occasionally overlapping loyalties. For example, a 20-something returning from Afghanistan ready to enroll in college under the new Post-9/11 G.I. Bill may find little in common personally and politically with a World War II veteran receiving Medicare.

Importantly, the respective concerns of each of these groups are very much dependent upon how "their" war was perceived by the public. For instance, World War II-era veterans, roughly one-third of the then national male population over age 15, were heralded as the Greatest Generation (Department of Veterans Affairs, 2004). Contrarily, the U.S. involvement in Korea has been colloquially dubbed the Forgotten War and Vietnam veterans struggled for decades before the engagement was "upgraded" from conflict to war. Veterans of OEF/OIF will likely enjoy a more modest version of the appreciation shown to their WWII-era counterparts.

If for no other reason, this is attributable to the fact that, like the Second World War, the Global War on Terror was at least initially perceived by most Americans to be an act of reactive self-defense, rather than an intrusive peace-keeping or stability operation. This was obviously not the case during the nation's several decades spent combatting the spread of Communism. In some ways, this is illustrative of a pluralized conflict as soldiers have served in a plethora of often unrelated conflicts, generally separated by years of peace (Harper & Leicht, 2011, p. 54). Consequently, the changes in perception of PTSD have been slow and piecemeal.

The current place of the veteran in American society is unique to these times. In his famous essay, retired Army Lieutenant Colonel and Professor of Military Science Dave Grossman (2000) explained the relationship between what he perceived as the three major social roles assumed by individuals relative to safety and security; sheep, wolves, and sheepdogs. Therein, the majority of people are sheep. They are gentle, unassuming, and could only harm another by accident or under extreme provocation. Conversely, the wolves prey on the sheep without mercy. Therefore, it is the duty of the sheepdogs to protect the flock. However, the sheepdog looks very similar to the wolf; which does not go unnoticed by the sheep. He has fangs and is capable of visiting violence upon others. This frightens the sheep. They shun the sheepdog because he does not belong. Yet, when the wolves come, the sheep rally behind the sheepdog. In a more narrow sense than Grossman intended, veterans represent the sheepdogs of our society. More importantly, they remind the populace of the unpleasantness endured by some so that the many may prosper; the thin blue shell that protects the delicate life inside the robin's egg.

Therefore, the veteran is socially isolated. This is particularly true if he or she suffers from a visible or invisible injury that may remind the sheep of the atrocity of war. Fortunately, the historical and anecdotal data is sufficient to paint a longitudinal picture of how Western, specifically American, civilization evolved (or perhaps degenerated) into a mass society and illustrate what impact this has had on returning warriors.

In Mythology and Ancient History through the Renaissance

Emotional responses to trauma have been documented in some of the most ancient religious texts, allegories, and moral lessons. For example, the compilation of Indian mythology called the *Mahabharata* chronicles a great war said to have taken place in 3139 BCE. It contains graphic depictions of numerous battles and described vivid combat stress reactions displayed by the warrior characters (Jayatunge, 2012). Similarly, the Buddhist Jataka stories, compiled between the 3rd Century BCE and 5th Century CE, contain some of history's oldest fables. Throughout these tales, numerous characters conveyed symptoms consistent with PTSD; such as a monk who suffered from hyper-vigilance, avoidance, and emotional detachment (Davids, 1880).

To Westerners, the Book of Job is the Holy Bible details what is perhaps the most well-known account of human suffering. The story portrays a man who endured a gauntlet of psychological stressors and disappointment in order to highlight the resilience of the human spirit; within the framework of what Carl Jung (1952/2010) would later term the "divine drama." Subsequently, researchers have contended that Job's mental anguish and reactions were comparable in many respects to the symptoms often observed in people suffering from PTSD (Haughn & Gonsiorek, 2009).

Some of the most prominent works of classical literature are permeated with references to the psychological and emotional impact of combat. Perhaps most poetically, Homer's (730 BCE / 1998) epic, *The Iliad*, provides intimate accounts of battles stress; the most notable of which are the lamentations of survivor's guilt proclaimed by the archetypical warrior Achilles following the death and desecration of his friend

Patroclus (p. 270). Homer also described the curious actions of Ajax, who went mad under Athena's spell and slaughtered an entire herd of sheep that he mistook for the enemy before ultimately killing himself (p. 303). Notably, the poem uniquely presented the agony of separation endured by the Trojan women while their husbands, brothers, and sons were embattled.

Undoubtedly, future poets and playwrights were influenced by this image of military wives and war widows as indirect victims of armed conflict. This is especially evident in the pleas of a soldier's wife taken from Shakespeare's (1597 / 2010) Henry IV, Part I: "In thy faint slumbers I by thee have watched, and heard thee murmur tales of iron wars...Thy spirit within thee hath been so at war and thus hath so bestirred thee in thy sleep" (Act II, Scene III). Written over four centuries ago without the insight of even rudimentary psychiatric knowledge, these lines infer the onslaught of symptoms such as sleep disturbance and flashback dreams. It is also axiomatic in the dialogue throughout this scene that the soldier suffers from social withdrawal, depression, and problems with intimacy. Ultimately, his wife reasons that if he does not care enough to tell her what troubles him, he must not love her. Surely today, some veterans' wives cry similar pleas into the night.

Shakespeare (1603 / 1993) affixed descriptions of psychological disorder to many of his most famous characters. Recall that his Scottish Army General, Macbeth, suffered hallucinations and nightmares as he became overwhelmed with guilt after, with the aid of his wife, he devised and executed a plot to kill King Duncan in order to facilitate his own selfish aspirations. Even Lady Macbeth displayed comorbid symptoms of dissociation and obsessive-compulsive behavior afterward as she began to sleepwalk and continually wring her hands, to make them clean, until she took her own life.

In times barely removed from feudalism, when the preponderance of men were intimately or otherwise familiar with pain and interpersonal violence, great writers took the dysfunctions observed in their fellow men and applied them to their characters. Subsequently, the observer was presented with a situation where an otherwise powerful and rational human being succumbed to the horrors of his/her own psyche. These are necessarily quite intimate narratives that allowed readers to connect with the ailing warriors; not comparable in any way to the common "tough guy" image of today's cinematic fiction.

Regardless of the available literature which conveyed that combat stress was quite natural, at this time and for centuries hence, soldiers were nonetheless held to an archaic standard of mental toughness. This expectation was eloquently outlined by the French knight Geoffroi de Charny in his 14th Century treatise *The Book of Chivalry.* Therein, the author warned young soldiers that they would see people killing each other, fleeing, dying, and being taken prisoner and that their friends would die beside them. He cautioned that it may be tempting to escape in dishonor on the backs of their horses, but that he who stays would win eternal honour. In order to defeat the melancholy associated with combat hardships, such as sleep deprivation, hunger, and exhaustion, Charny prescribed an unyielding devotion to chivalric duty and faith in God (Kaeuper & Kennedy, 1996). One can only speculate as to the efficacy of this treatment.

Military doctors made the first concerted attempts to categorize and diagnose the manifestations of acute combat reaction for which Johannes Hofer had championed the term "nostalgia" in his 1688 medical dissertation. This classification survived through the end of the Seven Years War and described the disorder as consisting of depression, angst, and exhaustion. Since the symptoms were believed to be associated with soldier's longing to return home during extended campaigns (not to actual battlefield experiences), both the French and Germans classified the malady as "homesickness"; *maladie du pays* and *heimweh* respectively. In Spain, the same symptoms would come to be known as *estar roto* ("to be broken"). This notion persisted through much of the Napoleonic era (Charvat, 2010).

Non-Combat Related PTSD

It is important to note that post-traumatic stress reactions to crises are not, nor have they ever been, quarantined to the field of battle. Though war veterans often have unique experiences compared to those of their civilian contemporaries, debilitating psychological ailments are a common adaptive response to traumatic events. There are myriad forms of stress which can manifest into hysterical reactions consistent with the clinical diagnoses of PTSD. The commonality therein is that wherever and however they occur, the events must be catastrophic stressors outside the scope of normal human experience (American Psychiatric Association, 2000). However, before the dawn of psychiatry, neurologists simply labeled various post-traumatic syndromes according to the nature of the event which precede the onset of symptoms in feeble attempts to establish causation.

In 19th Century Victorian Britain, as advancements in transportation and communication were bringing the world together like never before, survivors of railway accidents often reported suffering from chronic and severe anxiety. Many were subsequently diagnosed with "railway spine," which was accompanied by fatigue, trembling, and anxiety. In 1865, famed author Charles Dickens reported such symptoms after being involved in a railway accident in England (Dickens, 1880 / 2008).

At the time, it was believed that the condition was the result of a violent impact to the nerves within the spine. However, a French neurologist, Jean-Martin Charcot, introduced the notion of an underlying neurological disease known as hysteria, which was quickly abandoned by mainstream medical professionals. Though time would reveal that Charcot happened to be on the right track, his theory was avoided due to the concurrent rise of welfare reform in Europe.

Germany had very recently become the first country to offer state-funded disability compensation. Consequently, a psychologist by the name of CTJ Rigler coined the term "compensation neurosis," popular among railroad lawyers, as a comprehensive placeholder for these cases; with "compensation" referring to a new law which allowed people to sue for damages as a result of emotional suffering (Rosen, pp. 214-216). He and others regarded such traumatic symptoms as the inventions of a litigious bunch of malingerers. Therefore, this represents a transitional period wherein the people simultaneously handed-off responsibility to government and industry, while distancing themselves from their fellow citizens. Given the "macho" nature of their occupation, veterans would find even more difficulty in having stress reactions recognized as legitimate disabilities.

The Birth of Modern Warfare

The evolution of public perception in American society regarding veterans who suffer from PTSD resembles Foucault's (1961/1965) analysis of insanity throughout the development of Western civilization. He wrote of the Ships of Fools into which insane persons were corralled and sent adrift. As Leprosy had only recently vanished, the mad assumed the social role of the leper. During the Renaissance era, there was a certain amount of romance attached to the notion of an emotionally unstable and abandoned individual finding his peace with nature and the Judeo-Christian god (pp. vi-vii, 7-8).

These sentiments were transplanted and survived into the more volatile years of the United States. For instance, unit medical staffs became utterly overwhelmed during the American Civil War as thousands of troops were diagnosed with "soldier's heart." The Union Army alone reported more than 5,200 cases of "nostalgia" and another 2,600 diagnoses of insanity; both of which are likely gross underestimates (Charvat, 2010). Subsequently, many of the afflicted were placed in rail cars with the name of their home towns or states pinned to their uniforms. Others were simply sent to wander the countryside until they succumbed to thirst, hunger, or exposure (Bentley, 2005). If they could have been ignored, perhaps they would have been collectively forgotten.

Importantly, it was around the end of the War Between the States that citizens became moved (or at least aggravated) by the plight of their warriors. According to Bentley (2005), the legion of wandering veterans became such a cause for concern that public demand prompted the establishment of the first American military hospital for the insane in 1863. Therein, the people deflected personal responsibility for their veterans, which is quite astonishing considering that the war had been fought on American soil and, in some cases, literally in citizens' backyards.

With President Lincoln's promise, the federal government assumed an official stance in caring for the nation's veterans; though psychological reactions to combat were still not accepted as legitimate disabilities. Rather, the hospital was regarded as a sort of halfway house for traumatized veterans until they could be claimed by a family member. Similarly, Foucault (1961 /1965) alluded to the use of the Commandery of Saint Louis which was to be used as a rest home for military invalids, but wherein the insane were also confined (p. 39).

Technological advances continued to make each generation of soldiers the most accurate and destructive up to that point in history. Consequently, psychological stress reactions became exceedingly prevalent to the point of being unmanageable. Nevertheless, most military commanders and politicians continued to believe that hysterical reactions to trauma were indicative of a lack of discipline; contending that those who suffered from such symptoms were malingerers.

Though the concept had existed previously, Pierre Janet became the first to clearly explain that dissociation was a direct psychological defense against overwhelmingly stressful experiences and that it plays an important role in post-traumatic stress responses (van der Kolk, Brown, & van der Hart, 1989). However, this information did not travel in any expeditious manner through the impermeable layers of bureaucracy. Nonetheless, during its war with Japan in 1905, the Russian Army became the first in history to affirm that mental breakdown, a.k.a. "battle shock," shared a causal relationship with combat stress.

Military psychiatry was born with Russia's attempts to diagnose and treat battle shock; which resulted in roughly 2 of every 10 afflicted soldiers being deemed capable of returning to the front (Gabriel, 1987, pp. 109-112). This was a remarkable progressive move toward recognition of battlefield stress as a legitimate ailment; even if the ultimate goal was merely to return soldiers to combat quickly. Nonetheless, such advances in treatment would remain decades in the future for "malingering" American troops.

The uniquely brutal nature of trench warfare in World War One brought combat stress and governmental ignorance to the forefront. One of the most disturbing examples occurred when 300 British soldiers suffering from battlefield trauma were executed for cowardice. It would be nearly one hundred years before the United Kingdom would grant them posthumous pardons (BBC, 2006). Rather than build upon the compendium of extant medical literature concerning the link between battlefield trauma and psychological disorder, researchers of the era started from scratch and initially attributed the condition to the new weaponry of war; namely large-caliber artillery and explosives.

The unfounded belief that the impact of shells produced concussions capable of disrupting neural function birthed the term "shell shock"; an obvious confusion of correlation with causation. Ultimately, about 8% of all troops sent to fight in Europe were removed from action for psychological reasons. By the end of WWI, clinicians began to realize that shell shock was not actually caused by physical damage to the brain. However, it was still widely believed that such conditions only afflicted men of exceptionally weak character. Utilizing a different approach than their predecessors, yet arriving at the same near-sighted conclusion, physicians contended that the solution was to develop more thorough military entrance screening processes. Particular attention was paid to sifting through draftees in order to mediate the potential for emotional breakdown. With the aid of psychiatric testing, the military rejected some five million men from service on this presumption (Mitchell, 2010).

The late historian and former World War Two-era Army platoon commander, Paul Fussell (1989), explained that "the allied war has been sanitized and romanticized almost beyond recognition" particularly because it is commonly viewed as a just war (p. ix). Importantly, these stories significantly influence how observers regard veterans of these conflicts. What is particularly shocking about the lack of knowledge concerning combat stress in the Second World War is that it was so incredibly rampant, yet almost comprehensively ignored. Most famously, during his visit to a field hospital in Sicily in 1943, U.S. Army General George S. Patton slapped a young soldier who had been hospitalized for battle fatigue. Thereafter, Patton is reported to have proclaimed "I won't have the hospitals cluttered up with these sons of bitches who haven't got the guts to fight. Send that yellow son of a bitch back to the front line." This brand of machismo and disregard for troop welfare led to numerous afflicted servicemen having "lack of intestinal fortitude" annotated in their military service records (Gandolfini, 2010).

According to Bentley (2005), of the roughly 800,000 soldiers who actually saw combat during WWII, 37.5% displayed such severe symptoms of combat stress that they were permanently discharged; which is an absolutely staggering statistic. In the U.S. Army alone (not including the Air Corps) over 500,000 men were removed from the front indefinitely and nearly 1.4 million more temporarily for psychiatric reasons. As it was difficult to believe that so many of the Greatest Generation were encumbered by "weak" characters, the military adopted the practice of employing sterilized euphemistic language and stopped questioning individual fortitude. Consequently, the condition was referred to as "battle fatigue."

By the time that the United States intervened in Korea, the humanity of combat stress had been almost completely removed and its perceived seriousness diminished. Those displaying symptoms of traumatic reactions were said to have suffered from "operational exhaustion," which further distanced observers from the reality of the disorder. Of the nearly 200,000 soldiers who saw combat during the Korean War, nearly one-quarter were classified as psychiatric casualties.

No More Vietnams

It is no longer a topic of debate that the fighting during the Vietnam War was demonstrably more intense than was experienced in previous American conflicts; largely due to the mobility of the helicopter which kept troops almost perpetually embattled. Unfortunately, as asserted by former President Richard Nixon, the Vietnam War "was misreported then, and it is misremembered now" (Nixon, 1985, p. 9). The conflict and the men who fought it remain among the most misunderstood in American history.

From the outset of the Vietnam War, the military employed various preventive measures to decrease the number of psychological casualties, such as providing every battalion with medical staff trained in the identification and treatment of specific mental health problems. In the initial years of the war, these protocols appeared to be largely successful. However, this was a new kind of conflict. Americans were not only fighting the North Vietnamese Army (NVA), but the mostly unidentified Viet Cong (VC) as well. Undoubtedly, the notion of an unknown enemy was particularly taxing on their psychological well-being.

Moreover, soldiers in Vietnam were the first to be given a date of expected return from overseas (DEROS). This alone hindered the development of the usual buffers against combat stress, such as unit cohesion. One-year individual tours prevented many troops from feeling as if they were truly part of something larger than themselves and hampered group morale. As the war progressed and the public began to question its legitimacy, instances of combat reaction increased (Bentley, 2005). This was the first time in American history that many citizens welcomed their veterans as murderers rather than heroes.

Veterans returning from the campaign who displayed symptoms of psychological trauma were said to be suffering from Post-Vietnam Syndrome, which consisted of combat-related nightmares, depression, alcohol and drug dependence, and/or anxiety. However, the malady was not recognized by the APA and the U.S. Government contended that it was merely a "transient situational disorder"; hence regarded as a pre-existing condition and not eligible for treatment or compensation through the Department of Veterans Affairs (VA).

In 1979, eight long years after it was initially proposed, having been killed and reincarnated several times, Senator Alan Cranston's bill which called for the establishment of outreach centers for Vietnam veterans suffering from service-related psychological problems was passed by Congress. It wasn't until the following year that Post-Traumatic Stress Disorder was finally recognized by the mental health community in the Diagnostic and Statistical Manual of Mental Disorders Version III (DSM-III). Factual estimates of the prevalence of combat stress reactions vary, but the oft-cited National Vietnam Veterans' Readjustment Study, conducted by Congressional mandate in 1983, concluded that nearly one-third of Vietnam veterans have had PTSD at some point in their lives and that some 830,000 suffered from PTSD at the time of the study. However, only about 55,000 had filed relevant disability claims; roughly half of which had been upheld by adjudication boards (Price, 2007).

Summary and Conclusions

Though its name has changes over the ages, the construct known since 1980 as Post-Traumatic Stress Disorder has been documented since scholars first sought to explain human behavior. Medical professionals spent centuries haphazardly seeking the underlying causes of the condition, but were ultimately limited by their physiological model of medicine until the emergence of psychoanalysis. The place-holders used to describe the disorder were merely physicians' attempts to create broadly descriptive syndromes based upon unreliable self-reports and confused causation. As in the time of the Ships of Fools, sane men have had difficulty accepting that not much separates them from madness.

Following the Vietnam War and the belated acceptance of Post-Traumatic Stress Disorder as a legitimate disability, the public appears to have agreed with the use of their tax dollars to treat veterans suffering from PTSD. However, weakening solidarity has served to shift the responsibility for treatment to the bureaucracy of government. Ostensibly, Americans do not necessarily feel that veterans are literally fighting for them or their individual freedoms. Rather, they defend a more abstract concept of national interest which may or may not have anything to do with the observer.

In a society wherein so few choose to serve, veterans are susceptible to stigmatization due to a lack of understanding of their experiences. It may be difficult for someone to relate to a particular issue if he or she does not personally know anyone connected to it. Ergo, public ignorance can prompt myths concerning the stability and worthiness of veterans as well as erect social barriers toward seeking professional assistance. This is becoming especially true as the United States has remained almost perpetually at war or in preparation for one since at least the early 1900s.

Under such circumstances, those who do not actually participate in the conflict may become detached from the media sound bites as the live feed of explosions in some distant land becomes business as usual. Much like Fussell's aforementioned analysis of the Second World War, the current War on Terror has been romanticized. The role formerly filled by John Wayne in his Kevlar helmet with unbuckled chinstrap is being assumed by young chiseled men in countless films. This provides a completely skewed idea of what war is and how it affects the human mind. Where advancements in transportation and social welfare reform prompted dramatic changes in how those suffering from combat stress in the 19th Century were perceived, mass communications continue to detach citizens from the reality of Post-Traumatic Stress Disorder.

Part Four:
International, Human & Civil Rights Law

XI

Addressing the Use of Sexual Violence as a Strategic Weapon of War

Sexual violence has been employed as a strategic weapon of war for at least as long as historians have been documenting conflicts. Indeed, members of nearly every standing army in history have participated in some form of rape warfare (Vikman, 2005). Consequently, the international community has implemented various forms of legislation which criminalize the deliberate targeting of civilians during armed conflict (Bergoffen, 2006; Haddad, 2011). Nonetheless, rape remains one of the most under-reported and inadequately prosecuted of all war crimes (Falcon, 2001).

Certainly, a lack of discipline exhibited by inexperienced and non-professional warriors in tribal conflicts can explain a fraction of these occurrences. Though, it would be disingenuous to affix such justifications upon those instances which were deliberately calculated by the professional warfighters and commanders of comparably advanced armies (Valenius, 2004). Moreover, the sheer prevalence of its use precludes the validity of the "bad apple" argument, wherein a deviant minority becomes the scapegoat which suffers for the sins of an apathetic organization (Whitmer, 2006). Indeed, sexual deprivation and base desire cannot explain why even educated military strategists would advocate the use of sexual violence in warfare. Unless, of course, they regard it as an invaluable weapon which strategically targets the psychological well-being and social cohesion of civilian populations as well as the morale of enemy units (Clifford, 2008).

In order to address the resultant social problems associated with sexual violence in conflict, it is necessary to understand the motivations and intent behind the groups that have sanctioned its use. Those who have used rape as a weapon perceive it to be an effective complimentary method by which their goals can be achieved and are drawn to its symbolic message of dominance (Baaz & Stern, 2009). Accordingly, those who wish to remedy its negative consequences and mediate future occurrences must understand why it works in the first instance (Mukamana & Brysiewicz, 2008).

Most importantly, careful study of the underlying justifications for its use may reveal avenues by which these motivations can be arrested or removed (Dwyer, 2009). If such inclinations cannot be combatted, viable deterrence measures may be implemented which will raise the cost to the perpetrators of rape warfare beyond its potential benefit to their cause (Castillo, 2007). Recent landmark rulings represent small steps toward resolution via the adjudication of wartime rapists. Regardless, victims' advocates remain largely unimpressed; many having become even more vocal in their demands for justice (Bergoffen, 2006; Hargreaves, 2001). Therefore, the need for a victim-focused humanitarian response is axiomatic. Even when copiously applied, the law alone cannot cure the social plights which disproportionately affect women and children in the wake of wartime atrocity (Ghobarah, Huth, & Russett, 2003).

The History and State of Rape Warfare

The prevalence of sexual violence in warfare is well documented and permeates world history. According to Gottschall (2004), its use was illustrated in ancient texts such as Homer's *Iliad* and the Old Testament of the Holy Bible (e.g. *Zechariah 14:2*). In the 13th Century, Genghis Khan established specific policies which encouraged the use of rape warfare as he expanded his empire. Khan infamously proclaimed that one of the greatest pleasures in life was to ravage the daughters and wives of one's enemies (Clifford, 2008).

Rape was later employed as a strategic weapon by members of both the Allied and Axis armies during World War II as a means to terrorize civilian populations and demoralize their respective enemies (Epp, 1997; Ferraro, 2008). The most atrocious example within this era was the infamous Japanese campaign which became known as the Rape of Nanking. After killing about half of the city's approximated 600,000 residents, Japanese Imperial Army soldiers gang-raped between 20,000 and 80,000 Chinese females of various ages (Sedgwick, 2009). Therein, fathers were forced to rape their daughters and sons their mothers, generally under threat of death, while other family members watched (Zimbardo, 2007, pp.16-17). Ostensibly, this was a calculated employment of psychological warfare aimed at reducing the cohesion of family units and the community as a whole so that Japanese authority would not be resisted (MacDonald, 2005; Sedgwick, 2009).

More recently, sexual violence has become a component of civil warfare in developing nations such as Afghanistan and Guatemala, as well as amid the purported 400,000 deaths associated with state-sponsored genocide in the Darfur region of Sudan (Hagan, Rymond-Richmond, & Parker, 2005). Though rape warfare has endured into the modern era, sexual violence is still perceived by many to be an inherent byproduct of war itself; influenced by such factors as the sexual deprivation of mobilized troops, a lack of military discipline, and the biological drive to produce offspring (Clifford, 2008; Thornhill & Palmer, 2000; Vandermassen, 2011).

This indifference only perpetuates its use and lessens the likelihood that perpetrators will face justice for their transgressions. Moreover, such callous assertions are void of empirical evidence and cannot explain the rampant and coordinated use of sexual violence (Buss, 2009; Clifford, 2008). Rape warfare is as old as written human history, having been employed by uneducated tribesman and military tacticians alike (Clifford, 2008; Gottschall, 2004). However, advancements in military technology seem to have replaced or improved upon virtually every aspect of armed conflict, save for two of man's baser desires; sex and violence.

The Efficacy of Sexual Violence as a Weapon

Sexual violence is a common thread in modern conflicts and genocidal operations in the Third World (Clifford, 2008). Two contemporary examples of the state-sponsored coordinated use of rape warfare were perpetrated against "out groups" of Bosnia-Herzegovina from 1992-95 and of Rwanda in the spring of 1994 (Haddad, 2011; Staub, 1999; Weitsman, 2008). In addition to being a psychological weapon, rape warfare was used therein with the deliberate intention of significantly diminishing particular ethnic populations. In both instances, governmental approval offered a license for sadistic innovation against the targeted populations (Jamieson, 1999).

Such was the nature of its employment during a tribal conflict between the Hutu and Tutsi communities of Rwanda. Amid an estimated 800,000 to 1 million deaths, roughly three-quarters of the entire Tutsi population was eradicated (Leitenberg, 1994; Mukamana & Brysiewicz, 2008). This state-sponsored genocide operation armed the Hutu populations and encouraged them to use rape as a tactic of terror and spiritual annihilation. One Hutu leader, Mayor Silvester Cacumbibi, is rumored to have told one of his victims "We won't waste bullets on you; we will rape you and that will be worse for you" (Zimbardo, 2007, p. 13).

One of the largest mass rape-murders of a Tutsi population during this conflict was orchestrated by Pauline Nyiramasuhuko, a former social worker, minister, and lecturer on female empowerment who was herself a Tutsi (Hogg, 2010). Therein, Nyiramasuhuko created a ruse wherein she convinced the Tutsi people within the village of Butare to gather for a humanitarian aid drop, whereupon they were cut down by automatic weapons, grenades, and machetes. She ordered the Hutu aggressors to rape all of the women before killing them (Durkham & O'Byrne, 2010; Zimbardo, 2007, p. 13). When the men became fatigued, she provided gasoline from her own vehicle so that the remaining women could be burned to death. One young Tutsi woman, Rose, was raped by Nyiramasuhuko's son who had received "permission" from his mother. After being forced to watch the rape of her own mother and the murders of several of her relatives, Rose was allowed to live so that she could "deliver a progress report" as a witness to the massacre (Zimbardo, 2007, p. 13).

Incidents such as this were not uncommon during the Rwandan tribal conflict. Researchers estimate that approximately 350,000 Tutsi females were raped within this three-month period (Bijleveld, Morssinkhof, & Smeulers, 2009). Military strategists may regard this activity as a waste of valuable resources and manpower. Moreover, troops would be potentially exposing themselves to venereal diseases while commanders run the risk of losing control of their men, making their units combat ineffective (Donovan, 2002; Meini, 2008). However, the Hutu leaders and sponsoring government understood the power of the message. To them, it was not counter-productive to kill women immediately after they were raped, so long as a select few lived to tell the story; women like Rose. Therefore, rape warfare exemplifies intimidation in its most malevolent form (Parfitt, 2004).

The efficacy of rape warfare has been substantiated through its implementation as a weapon by which warring factions have facilitated their goals (Clifford, 2008). However, the same could be said of concentration camps and the mass exterminations organized by the Nazi Party during the Second World War. One notable difference therein is that many of the perpetrators of the Holocaust were adjudicated at the Nuremberg Trials (Hoffman, 1999). Contrarily, those who have sanctioned and committed rape warfare have historically evaded justice (Falcon, 2001). For example, following a 36-year civil war in Guatemala, rape victims and their families maintained that absolute blame rested upon the state-sponsored soldiers who had perpetuated the barbarity. Nonetheless, they believed that their only available recourse was through legitimate state agents, whose power rivaled or superseded that of the offenders. Paradoxically, their demands for justice could only be heard by members of the same government that had initially mobilized the soldier-rapists (Hastings, 2002; Ross, 2004).

Similarly, sexual violence amid armed conflict in the Democratic Republic of the Congo has been labeled by the United Nations (UN) as a strategic weapon of war and a gross violation of human rights. Regardless, and in spite of the Goma peace agreement, the atrocities persisted unabated. Both state and non-state armed groups have been identified as perpetrators of rape warfare by the UN and declared to be in violation of various international laws, to include the Nuremberg Code. Nonetheless, the study of mass rape during armed conflict is largely done retrospectively, with significant intervention rarely taking place (Maedl, 2011).

These contemporary examples demonstrate that the perpetrators of rape warfare are largely immune from judicial proceedings. Indeed, even when an international body as powerful as the UN condemns their actions, offenders can be reasonably certain that they will never answer for their transgressions, which only buttresses their perceived entitlement to the "spoils" of war (Falcon, 2001; Mukamana & Brysiewicz, 2008). In the absence of cogent deterrence measures, rape warfare has become an omnipresent consequence of armed conflict (Clifford, 2008).

Injustice and Under-reporting

Among many populations, rape is the most underreported of all violent crimes, even during peacetime (Clay-Warner & McMahon-Howard, 2009; Falcon, 2001). Many rapes are not reported due to the victims' lack of understanding of what legally constitutes a sexual assault. Therein, ignorance of the law breeds trepidation. Moreover, survivors often perceive that they will be somehow further victimized by law enforcement personnel or the judicial system (Clay-Warner & McMahon-Howard, 2009).

This preconception has been reinforced by numerous historical examples and will require significant action to remedy. Additionally, victims often feel embarrassed and wish to keep the incidents private as they question their own culpability (Clay-Warner &

McMahon-Howard, 2009; S. Holmes & R. Holmes, 2009, pp. 218-219). In roughly 10 percent of cases, this embarrassment eventually manifests as shame, largely due to fear of public scrutiny and cultural ideologies which tend to at least partially blame the victim for the assault (Weiss, 2010). Victims must first understand that they have suffered from a crime that is punishable by law and that the perpetrators bear the full burden of guilt. More importantly, they must have access to justice (Allen, 2007). Ergo, an effective counter strategy must incorporate the application of human-rights law and humanitarian advocacy.

Framework of International Law

The practice of rape warfare is diametrically opposed to the principles conveyed in customary international law. According to Kauzlarich & Kramer (1998), the first of these has been upheld since the 1907 Hague Conventions in that both combatants and noncombatants are protected from unnecessary and aggravated suffering. Secondly, distinction must always be made between combatants and civilians (p. 26). Subsequently, the 1948 Genocide Convention prohibited the conspiracy, attempt, complicity, incitement, and/or actual execution of genocide or "ethnic cleansing." Moreover, the 1949 Geneva Conventions (I-IV) specifically condemned violence to life or person and mutilation, as well as the cruel treatment and torture of combatants and civilians (p. 23). Perhaps even more importantly, the Nuremberg Charter explicitly demonized crimes against humanity, such as inhumane acts committed against civilians, regardless of whether or not the violation is considered a crime according to the law of the nation wherein it was perpetrated (p. 32). Such humanitarian principles were intentionally applied to armed conflicts as expressed in the United Nations General Assembly Resolution 244 (XXIII) of 1965 (p. 26).

Accordingly, there is a significant legal framework within which to prosecute war criminals who have condoned or practiced rape warfare. However, history has shown that the deficiency lies in enforcement (Clifford, 2008). The International Criminal Court (ICC) has been repeatedly criticized by feminist scholars as being virtually impotent in the prosecution of rape warfare perpetrators. Only recently has the ICC begun to investigate and indict, though most cases rarely evolve beyond the investigation phase (Halley, 2008). Fortunately, recent cases have demonstrated an improving trend in prosecution (Haddad, 2011; Malone, 2008).

The sheer heinousness of violent sex crime is a sufficient catalyst to conjure public demand for the persecution of offenders from victims, advocates, and concerned citizens (Winnick, 2008). Provided there is sufficient pressure, this inevitably translates into political necessity for those who wish to maintain their station (Barker, 2007). For example, though sex offenders comprised an insignificant portion of overall arrests in the United States, their rate of incarceration has increased some 15% since 1980; higher than the rate for any other contemporary violent crime. Public demand is almost entirely responsible for this trend; and so can it be in the case of rape warfare (S. Holmes & R. Holmes, 2009, p. 275).

Relevant international human-rights and criminal laws are already in place (Kauzlarich & Kramer, 1998, pp. 23, 26, 32). However, the need for adequate awareness, education, and access remains. A victim who understands that he or she has suffered a sexual assault as defined under international law is comparably more likely to report the crime (Allen, 2007; Spohn & Horney, 1996). However, this will only happen if policy makers and legislators can convey through judicious action that these laws are taken seriously and properly enforced.

The Hague hosted the Yugoslav war-crimes tribunal, which specifically investigated the use of rape and sexual slavery as a means of ethnic cleansing during the 1992-95 Bosnian war (Thornberry, 1996). Therein, in accordance with the aforementioned customary principles, a judge sentenced three soldier-rapists to a combined term of 60 years for what he regarded as acts of utter disrespect for the victims' dignity and violations of fundamental human rights (Hargreaves, 2001).

This demonstrates that crimes against humanity, such as rape warfare, transcend local and even national jurisdictions. Moreover, they are no longer regarded as mere violations of international war rules. Rather, they are to be individually assessed as crimes under human-rights law (Askin, 1999; Haddad, 2011). Rulings such as this offer hope to the countless survivors who have suffered sexual assaults amid the turmoil of armed conflict. However, many feminists and victims' advocates condemned the Yugoslav decision as being far too lenient (Hargreaves, 2001). In reality, the recent International Criminal Tribunal rulings have produced equitable sentences under notoriously vague and misleading international humanitarian laws (Askin, 1999). What these advocates are truly expressing is discontent with the resultant "justice" brought forth by the enforcement of these codes. Indeed, a victim remains victimized whether or not his or her attacker is adjudicated. They are asking for something more.

The Humanitarian Approach

The international community must continue to enforce human-rights law, lest its authority be undermined. This is the first step toward implementing deterrence measures which may prevent future abuses (Askin, 1999; Haddad, 2011). As it is virtually impossible to avert all instances of rape warfare, abuses must be immediately recognized when they occur. Unlike the judicial process, such a strategy focuses on victims and potential victims rather than solely on perpetrators (Shanks & Schull, 2000). It is unlikely that any powerful nation or coalition will readily intervene in a tribal conflict in the absence of economic or strategic interests. Therefore, combating the social consequences of rape warfare on the ground remains primarily within the realm of humanitarian agencies and their healthcare professionals (Bristol, 2006).

The cogent humanitarian response necessitates a comprehensive intervention protocol. The immediate physical effects of sexual assault must be treated medically. Beyond simple triage, this includes the administration of antibiotics, screening for sexually-transmitted diseases, and emergency contraception (Shanks & Schull, 2000). Moreover, psychological support and counseling should be accessible to victims since emotional problems often manifest in the aftermath of sexual assault. It is advisable that referrals for these services be issued out by the medical first responders (Koss, 1993). This is especially important given that the period of two years following the attack is often the most traumatic time for victims (S. Holmes & R. Holmes, 2009, p. 259).

It is paramount that proper documentation be maintained and that avenues for reporting are accessible; not just in the immediate aftermath, but bearing in mind that a victim may decide to report at a later date. Accordingly, "rape kits" are an effective method by which physical evidence can be gathered and preserved. In combination with victim and eye-witness statements, a sufficient amount of evidence may be collected in order to facilitate criminal charges (Feldberg, 1997; Johnson, Peterson, Sommers, & Baskin, 2012). Thereby, the appropriate humanitarian response fulfills the basic requirements needed to pursue criminal prosecution.

Conclusion

Beyond the immediate physical effects, victims of rape experience intense emotional and psychological suffering long after the commission of the crime; often feeling ashamed, humiliated, and dehumanized. These intangible byproducts of sexual victimization impede the recovery process while simultaneously deterring victims from reporting (Allen, 2007; Koss, 1993). In addition to feeling totally helpless during the encounter, victims of sexual violence are often left with no available avenues by which to bring their aggressors to justice (Hastings, 2002). Consequently, rape remains one of the most underreported and subsequently under-prosecuted war crimes.

The decision not to report in such instances may be due to a lack of accessibility rather than a conscious choice (Falcon, 2001; Weiss, 2010). Indeed, a "fortunate" few may live to recount their stories to psychologists, criminologists, and other scholars so that their narratives may be added to the compendium of existing research. However, it remains unlikely that they or their attackers will ever see the inside of a courtroom as these crimes have historically gone unanswered in any meaningful way by the international community. The oft-repeated trend in most cases is that the innocent suffer while the trespasses of the wicked go unpunished (Clifford, 2008; Halley, 2008). These dire circumstances necessitate the simultaneous application of international law and humanitarian aid. Thereby, a preponderance of evidence and vocal advocacy will provide inertia for the movement which will bring rape warfare forever out of the shadows; where it can no longer be ignored.

XII

Intervention and Blowback: Examining the Use of Drone Strikes by American Forces in Pakistan through the Social Conflict Perspective

On Saturday, August 25, 2012, U.S. forces utilized unmanned aerial combat vehicles (drones) to execute five suspected militants in the northern Waziristan tribal area of Pakistan, near the Afghan border. This latest strike was part of a recent effort to dismantle the Haqqani militant network, a sect of which is believed to have been involved in several attacks on U.S. troops in Afghanistan. Many vocal Pakistanis contend that the drone program, managed by the Central Intelligence Agency (CIA), infringes upon the country's sovereignty. Contrarily, the American government maintains that drone strikes are an efficacious tool with which to combat terrorism and limit civilian casualties (Khan, 2012).

Citing national security concerns, the U.S. government did not officially admit that CIA drones were operating in Pakistan until May of 2012; in year nine of the program (Smith, 2012). Indeed, the most recent War Powers Resolution Report makes no mention of any military operations in Pakistan (Obama, 2012). However, the subsequently released data presented in Figure 1 shows that drone strikes have been actively pursuing targets therein since at least 2004 and in significantly greater volume since 2008. Currently, the broad U.S. definition of "militant" is a topic of contention and citizens of the Pakistani tribal areas claim that drones have been responsible for thousands of unreported civilian deaths. Figure 2 illustrates the controversial estimate of victim types killed in U.S. drone strikes since 2004. Interestingly, the number of "unknown" casualties seems to have increased as civilian deaths declined. Consequently, a Pakistani attorney, Shahzad Akbar, has initiated a legal campaign wherein he has filed law suits on behalf of drone strike victims against U.S. intelligence officials for carrying out the attacks and the Pakistani government for its allegedly apathetic position (Smith, 2012).

Figure 1. Reported Number of U.S. Drone Strikes in Pakistan

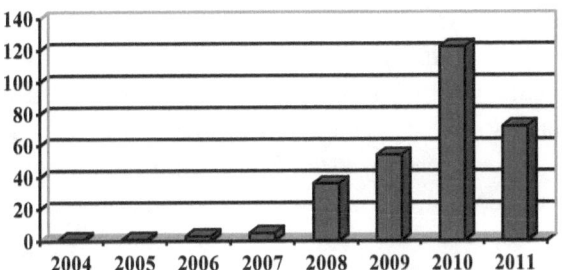

Figure 2. Estimated Types of Deaths from U.S. Drone Strikes in Pakistan
(Based on averages of annual high and low estimates)

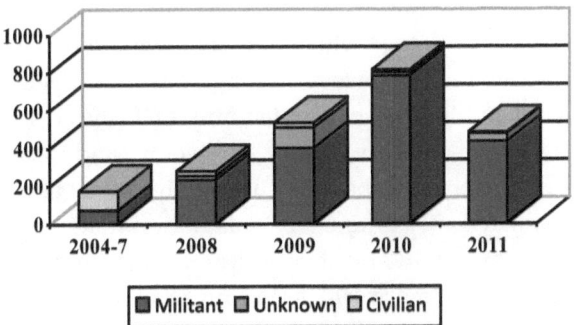

Gladwell (2011) noted that the U.S. military has progressed toward the ultimate goal of being able to "put a bomb inside a pickle barrel from 20,000 feet" since the World War II-era invention of the Norden MK-15 bombsight which was used to drop the "Little Boy" atomic bomb on Hiroshima, Japan. During Operation Enduring Freedom, the CIA has launched hundreds of drone strikes in northwest Pakistan and killed upwards of 2,000 suspected militants with a current accuracy rate of around 95 percent. However, since the inception of the drone program, the number of suicide and terrorist attacks against U.S. forces in Afghanistan has increased tenfold and anti-American sentiments permeate public discourse in Pakistan. Now that such amazing feats of target acquisition are technologically possible, contemporary guidance systems and drone craft have revealed how little this precision actually matters in the overall conflict resolution process. Regardless of accuracy, the larger problem has always been, not placing the ordinance, but knowing where to find the proverbial pickle barrel. More importantly, how should a nation use the weapons at its disposal and should it use them at all?

Main Assumptions and Principles of the Social Conflict Perspective

According to Ritzer (2011), the roots of the conflict perspective can be traced back to Hegelian-Marxian German sociology which initially regarded social facts as abstract ideas. However, Marx influenced a shift if this way of thinking by contending that social structures were the seat of many problems and that those structures must be overturned in order to facilitate change (p. 21). Ultimately, this notion materialized into the philosophy of the critical school, but remained outside of mainstream American social thought until the 1960s; undoubtedly linked to the concurrent rise of counter-culture (p. 58).

Subsequently, conflict theory was an answer, though a premature one, to the rampant criticism which targeted structural functionalism due to its inability to address social change and conflict (p. 60). Essentially, the conflict perspective shares an overlapping foundation with functionalism. Though, utopian notions of equilibrium were largely abandoned with the realization that conflict and tension existed between social structures (p. 62). The social conflict perspective views society as a perpetual struggle for scarce resources wherein the elite control the poor and marginalized, which is reminiscent of the evolutionary notion of finite ecological niches (pp. 133-134). Ultimately, the conflict perspective focuses on the negative nature of society and challenges the status quo by advocating social change and even revolution.

Karl Marx on Internationalism

In Marx's Ethnological Notebooks, written in the early-1880s just before his death, he repeatedly alluded to the viability of egalitarian forms of community as observed in the contemporary Third World. He contended that communal societies were often targeted by state agents who aimed to hinder their reproduction because they inherently opposed state forms of control (Gailey, 2003). The use of drone strikes in Pakistan does not appear to represent a means of controlling the tribal communities, though one is compelled to wonder if the perception of underdeveloped societies held by advanced nations serves as a means of justifying collateral damage and civilian casualties through dehumanization; a policy uncomfortably similar to Manifest Destiny.

Nonetheless, leaders of the Taliban and other Afghan extremist groups have long enjoyed a fiduciary relationship with the Pakistani government. Indeed, former Pakistani President Pervez Musharraf once affirmed that his hold on power depended upon continued governmental support of jihadist groups, which is illustrative of tension between social structures (Semple, 2012). Given that, in order to maintain some semblance of equilibrium, the Pakistani government has refused to impose military force in the Waziristan region, the actions of U.S. forces therein may represent a power grab for a seat of control and serve as an omnipresent reminder that America maintains firepower superiority.

Interestingly, Marxian ideology has become a significant component of contemporary theories on globalization; particularly those of the cultural variety. The current state of affairs in Pakistan may be indicative of cultural differentialism within a society which ostensibly wishes to refuse modernity and remain impervious to social change brought about by globalization (Ritzer, 2011, p. 77). Citizens of the remote frontier regions of Pakistan were historically shielded from exposure to opposing ideologies. Prior to American intervention, the tribal members of northern Pakistan very much constituted a class in itself. However, the realization of their conflicting relation to agents of the United States has catalyzed them into a true class for itself (p. 169).

This amelioration forged these Pakistanis into a social class which opposes U.S. intervention in their homeland. Notably, the conflict therein does not stem from competition over tangible resources, but from a struggle for power. Accordingly, Marx would likely view the citizens of Pakistan's tribal areas as representative of a marginalized communal society in need of social change. He would likely advocate a non-intervention U.S. policy in Pakistan and propose a revolution against the Pakistani government if needed. Though, in praxis such a strategy may result in the re-emergence of Taliban rule.

Marx's perspective has become somewhat anachronistic in warfare. His theories were developed in an age of empires wherein governments subdued dissenting citizens and maintained a physical foothold on their lands. Today, the tribal areas of Pakistan are haunted by a specter of fear in the form of unmanned drones; a sort of artificial state agent. That is not to say that Marx's theories are inapplicable; one simply needs to recognize that they are a remnant of their time and that the nature of war has changed a great deal since. Marx has much to offer by way of insight into armed conflict. However, the ability to control a region artificially from the safety of one's own borders may never have occurred to him.

Max Weber's Concept of Interest

According to Swedberg (2003), one of the most notable components of Max Weber's sociological theory is the concept of interest. These interests can be based on myriad social foundations; politics, economics, self, class, public, etc. Most importantly, interests are always shaped by society and virtually anything may become an interest through social force. He contended that the law is designed to protect not only economic interests, but other interests ranging from personal security to purely ideological notions of honor. Weber went so far as to state that interest is the dynamic which pushes action down the tracks determined by ideas (Weber, 1991, p. 280).

It seems plausible that the social push for vengeance against the perpetrators of the 9/11 terrorist attacks could have manifested into a public interest, which led the U.S. government to pursue Taliban targets not only in Afghanistan, but into the ally nation of Pakistan. Indeed, the phrase "national security" has peppered political discussion regarding the War on Terrorism. Moreover, the pursuit of this interest in the wake of thousands of American deaths has been used as a justification for resultant civilian deaths in Pakistan. Such noble cause justifications illustrate Weber's political ethic of "absolute ends" (Everett, 1997).

Though Weber's concept of interests and descriptions of political ethics are quite exceptional, they fall short of comprehensively explaining human behavior in modern war. For much the same reason as Marx's ideas, Weber's views on modernization cannot be applied to contemporary armed conflict during the Internet age. The modern world is becoming increasingly globalized as national borders are nearly obsolete. His theories of capitalism and economics appear to have maintained their applicability, but his concepts of domination do not seem to hold up to the weight of scrutiny today (Wong, 2000).

Conclusion and Reflection

Notably, the current American drone program as it operates in Pakistan is eerily similar to the pre-World War II notion of "morale bombing." However, contemporary social psychologists are well aware that attacking civilian populations with ordinance from largely unseen vessels serves only to bolster cohesion and improve morale among targeted populations (Anderson, 2010; Meilinger, 1996). Perhaps it is this phenomenon which has contributed to the formation of a marginalized class within Pakistan's tribal areas and the rise of anti-American sentiments therein. In any event, the current policy of indiscriminate drone strikes, however effective it may be in the short-term, is a perceived violation of national sovereignty and is therefore likely to produce a new crop of extremists who demonize the United States and seek revenge for any of myriad reasons, to include personal vengeance.

It seems unlikely that the social structures represented by the U.S. military and by the Pakistani tribesman will reach a peaceful equilibrium in lieu of a revolutionary change. Unfortunately, the very authority under which American forces operate in Pakistan is regarded as illegitimate by the affected citizenry. As affirmed by Arreguin-Toft (2006, p. 227), terrorists and insurgents will perpetually frustrate the U.S. so long as it supports corrupt regimes in the region, operates behind a shield of foreign policy double-standards, and refuses to employ means of resolution other than violence. In this vein, the immediate solution to eliminating threats against national security is fueling the extremist cause.

XIII

A Nation Divided: Civil War Politics and Emancipation

Abraham Lincoln certainly contemplated how history would illustrate his legacy. In hindsight, commentators and critics have regarded him as an opportunistic champion of civil rights and savior of democracy, as well as a tyrant and white supremacist (Cook, 2001; Dirck, 2009). Regardless of what has been written about him as a man and as a leader, his impact can best be discerned through the content of his own words and the intentions which guided his deeds. Was he truly the "Great Emancipator" as so many contend? Surely, an assessment of the legislation enacted under his administration qualifies him as worthy (McColley, 2005; Wilson, 2008). However, the sobriquet infers the single-minded objective of freeing a persecuted people and ignores the volatile political climate manifested within a nation bound for self-destruction.

Was he to sit in the highest office of a land wherein its citizens, all supposedly created equal in the eyes of their government, received such differential treatment? Undoubtedly, a humble man with such high regard for the law and unyielding hope for his country understood that the strength of the republic rested upon the merits of its citizens, whose fate may not be determined by birthright. Nevertheless, the romanticized narratives portraying Lincoln as savior ignore the social and political realities in which he found himself. Emancipation did not unite a people; it preserved a nation. The famous proclamation was an integral component of a desperate military strategy, not of a broader civil rights initiative, which ultimately intended to solidify the cogency of a seemingly impractical system of government.

In perhaps its darkest hour, Abraham Lincoln inherited custodianship of the great experiment in constitutional democracy which had set a precedent for the rest of the world; a nation in which the power was bestowed upon the people rather than a dictator, divine king, or priesthood. He was charged with leading a nation that was presently attempting suicide, yet reined it back from the brink of oblivion. The situation could best be described in the words of Harriet Tubman: "[L]iberty or death: If I could not have one, I would have the other" (Zinn, 2003, p. 132). More than the philosophy of a defiant iconoclastic woman, these sentiments conveyed the state of the republic near the end of the War Between the States as perceived by President Lincoln. Either it would be a society wholly comprised of free citizens or it would cease to exist in its intended form.

Economic and Racial Inequality

As the country unknowingly teetered on the precipice of internal conflict, slavery was treated with indifference by the ruling class and not yet regarded as a civil rights. Indeed, in 1857, the U.S. Supreme Court had ruled that the slave Dred Scott had no right to sue for his freedom, because he was not a person as defined by the Constitution, but mere property. Moreover, though successful in generating fear among rich whites, isolated rebellions were unlikely to prompt any lasting change (Zinn, 2003, p. 139). Why then, was the subject of slavery debated in the public sphere by members of the majority who were seemingly so far-removed from its effects? The inequality bred from slavery was not confined by ethnic borders. Rather, it evolved out of class warfare and distrust between the "haves" and "have-nots" of American society.

Segregation was employed by elitists with the collateral purpose of keeping poor whites and blacks from associating, and potentially sympathizing, with one another. An example of this occurred when Irish and Negro workers were separated during the construction of the Brunswick Canal in Georgia, due to fears that an insurrection would result if the two groups intermingled. Though infrequently, poor whites would encourage and aid rebellions in retaliation against slave owners out of resentment for their own economic plight. Subsequently, Draconian police responses were initiated against whites who fraternized across racial boundaries. Eventually, a remedy was adopted wherein poor whites were employed as overseers of black labor; granting them a certain degree of perceived authority over the Negro and propagating racial tensions, while simultaneously diverting the animosity away from the owners (Zinn, 2003, pp. 132-133). Thereby, segregation was a social control mechanism employed to maintain the status quo and secure profit.

Such a state of affairs is indicative of gross economic inequality, which was not confined to minority concerns of civil liberty. This conflict manifested within a socially constructed reality wherein members of marginalized groups forged alliances according to their socio-economic station, rather than on grounds of ethnicity. Slavery permitted the rich to grow ever wealthier while the poor toiled grudgingly, unable to compete in a market dominated by cheap labor and business interests. Only through the abolishment of slavery would upward social mobility become accessible and a viable middle class eventually materialize in the Land of the Free. As Frederick Douglas said, "What man can make, man can unmake." Consequently, President Lincoln appealed to the needs of businessmen and ambitious politicians in such a way that the slavery issue could be resolved; not by rebellion, but on terms established by the white majority (Zinn, 2003, pp. 135-139). Moreover, he could simultaneously please the emerging and politically active middle class; a demographic with whom he shared mutual empathy (Gienapp, 2002, p. 24).

Personal Sentiments and Political Realities

Like most men of his time, Lincoln did not necessarily regard blacks as equal persons. As a congressman in 1849, he proposed a resolution to abolish slavery in the District of Columbia, but included a mandate requiring local authorities to arrest and return fugitive slaves to their owners. During a Senate campaign speech given in Chicago, Illinois in July of 1858, Lincoln vehemently professed the ideal of a free nation wherein all men were created equal and treated as such. However, two months later in Charleston, South Carolina, he proclaimed that he was not, nor had ever been, "in favor of bringing about...the social and political equality of the white and black races." He supported the racial dichotomy of "superior and inferior" and was "in favor of having the superior position assigned to the white race." Subsequently, a common theme in his approach to abolition was to free the slaves and encourage their emigration to foreign countries (Zinn, 2003, p. 140).

Contemporary pundits would certainly regard such statements as thinly veiled hypocrisy. Nonetheless, one must understand the climate of pre-Civil War politics. It is unreasonable to suggest that any one set of principles would have sufficiently garnered support for a single candidate therein. Consequently, diverging opinions regarding slavery prompted the Northern and Southern factions of the Democratic Party to elect their own respective candidates for the 1860 presidential election;

Stephen A. Douglas and John C. Breckenridge (Gilmore, 2006).

Lincoln offered insight into his own personal revulsion of slavery when he declared that "If slavery is not wrong, nothing is wrong." However, he trusted in the law to prevent his personal beliefs from unduly influencing his political decisions and revealed the reality of his time by admitting that his Presidential authority did not grant him "an unrestricted right to act officially on this judgment and feeling" (Brands, 2009). Accordingly, Lincoln conceded that he would support an extension of slavery, just as he "would consent to any great evil, to avoid a greater one" (Gienapp, 2002, p. 52). To him, the greater evil was the specter of a divided nation.

President Lincoln did not approach the beginning of his tenure with the intention of pursuing emancipation. He affirmed in his March 1861 inaugural address that he would not interfere with the institution of slavery, citing his lack of lawful authority and personal inclination to do so; a stance parodied by Congress at the outset of the war. However, he wavered on this position so as to keep several slave states in the Union. This illustrates a perpetual and methodical assessment of political pressures from the radical elements of his weak coalition (Zinn, 2003, pp. 140-141).

These fluctuations were exploited by Frederick Douglas when he described the President's first years as unashamedly promotional of the welfare of the white majority and apathetic toward the rights of Negros (Brands, 2009). Regardless of Lincoln's attempts to appease, seven Southern states succeeded from the Union following his election to the Presidency. Convinced that diplomacy was temporarily impotent, he attempted to repossess the federal base at Fort Sumter, prompting the succession of four additional states (Zinn, 2003, p. 141). The Civil War had begun.

The War Between the States was not declared solely on the subject of slavery. However, many Union soldiers reasoned that only abolition could end the war and prevent similar conflicts from manifesting in the future (Manning, 2012). It is quite possible that Lincoln may never have broached the issue had it not become such a divisive topic and the military viability of the North not become so uncertain. Still, he did not approach emancipation from a civil rights perspective. Rather, he perceived it as a cogent method by which he could hasten an end to the conflict and ameliorate his country (Brands, 2009).

His concern was not for the plight of a particular minority, but for the implications inherent to fostering an equal society so blatantly hypocritical. More importantly, he realized that acquiescence would have harmed his credibility and perpetuated the slow death of his beloved Union. Without emancipation, the nation could not have survived in its intended democratic form. Subsequently, other marginalized peoples would have been increasingly hesitant to follow the American model by adopting individual liberty as a fundamental maxim.

The Confiscation Act of 1862 set the precedent for what would eventually evolve into the Emancipation Proclamation by granting freedom to all slaves fighting for the North. However, the law was not enforced by military commanders; a trend which the executive branch regarded with indifference. Even under pressure to increase enforcement, Lincoln made no such maneuver. Instead, the Confiscation Act served to quell the dissenting opinions of radical abolitionists without sacrificing his popularity among moderates.

In a letter response to a critic concerning the administration's impassive position, the President retorted that his "paramount objective...is to save the Union...not either to save or destroy Slavery." He elaborated that if possible, he would save the Union without freeing a single slave as readily as he would by freeing every last one (Zinn, 2003, p. 142). He cared only for the future of his nation. What Lincoln did not reveal in this letter, was that he had already drafted a preliminary emancipation order which was being deliberated among the members of his Cabinet (Brands, 2009).

The debate over emancipation of the slaves was born out of the South's refusal to believe that the President's true intention was to preserve the Union. Even abolitionists did not wholly accept that he would end slavery, though the prospect of emancipation was precisely why many of them supported him. These perceptions were largely constructed in response to Lincoln's reciprocal assault and defense of slavery during his campaign. However, his ostensibly hypocritical platform became necessary during the war in order to maintain support from Northern voters as well as appease the Border Slave States to avoid further fragmentation.

While contemplating the future of the war and the Union in a meeting with Quaker abolitionists, Lincoln expressed that a decree of emancipation was futile if improperly timed; stating that if such a proclamation could abolish slavery "John Brown could have done the work" (Brands, 2009). Therein, he conveyed that any piece of legislation was only as durable as the voter cohesion at its foundation. Lincoln never questioned the inherent inhumanity of slavery. He was merely being realistic in considering how the process of emancipation should be initiated.

Rather than immediately issue such a decree, President Lincoln began by proposing compensation to slaveholders for their loss of "property" so as to lessen the economic impact of abolition. As this program seemingly justified the ownership of human beings, he proposed it to his constituency by comparing the monetary cost of war to the cost of such compensation on taxpayers. He implored the Border State members of Congress to accept his deal while it was being offered, lest they lose the entire perceived value of their slaves as it was extinguished upon the military victory of the North. The representatives refused outright, primarily based upon their inability to determine exactly what would be done with their slaves following emancipation; a paradox contemplated by Lincoln himself.

Subsequently, he admitted to an assembly of freed slaves at the White House that their race was suffering "the greatest wrong inflicted on any people." However, he professed that even if given freedom, African-Americans would not obtain "equality with the white race." He simply could not envision an America wherein multiple races could co-exist as equals. Therefore, and as the slaves had not initially chosen to come to the United States, he encouraged their descendants to leave the country for Central America or Liberia; attempting to deflect the potential inequality through emigration (Brands, 2009).

Amid a dismal array of defeats suffered by the North, Lincoln viewed the Emancipation Proclamation as a drastic effort to redefine the Union mission and achieve victory. It was not born out of moral reflection nor reverence for individual liberty, but of military necessity. Accordingly, on the advice of Secretary of State William Seward, he tabled the decree pending a victory in battle so that it would not be viewed as a hopeless bluff or the death pangs of an exhausted force.

The time came following McClellan's disputable victory over Lee at Antietam Creek near Sharpsburg, Maryland on September 17, 1862. Though McClellan's 90,000 troops were unable to wholly defeat Lee's force of 50,000, Lee necessarily retreated. Five days later, the proclamation was published, declaring that all slaves shall be forever freed within the borders of the United States (Brands, 2009).

The Emancipation Proclamation produced its intended effect. In April of 1864, in response to unprecedented public demand, the Senate proposed the Thirteenth Amendment, which was affirmed by the House in January of the following year. The United States Government had officially declared an end to slavery on American soil. Notably, the legislation inspired more blacks to enter into the service of the Union army, transforming the meaning of the Civil War from preservation to liberation for many. Consequently, legions of the 4 million newly freed slaves deserted Southern plantations and became a potential force for whichever side could enlist them.

The Confederacy was at a crossroads; it could reach an amicable agreement with the slaves and employ them to prolong the conflict or surrender to the North and hope that the emancipation order could be renegotiated. Ultimately, the South acquiesced as blacks joined the Union cause in droves. As noted by James McPherson, "Without [the slaves'] help, the North could not have won the war as soon as it did, and perhaps...not have won at all" (Zinn, 2003, pp. 143-144).

Conclusion and Reflection

President Lincoln never intended to embark on a benevolent crusade to free his enslaved Negro countrymen. Rather, he methodically employed abolition as a means to improve the dire military situation of the North without alienating either his moderate or radical supporters. When the military success of the Union Army seemed most improbable, he proposed emancipation in order to redefine the meaning of the campaign and force the Confederacy into submission. Nonetheless, his ulterior motivations behind the proclamation did not lessen its profound impact. It was the nation's first quantifiable step away from hypocrisy and toward true equality. He successfully championed legislation which complimented his political and military objectives, while simultaneously adhering to his own personal moral convictions (Guelzo, 2002). Any president could have issued such a decree, but the notion of an equal society would have been irrelevant in an America divided by internal war. Through emancipation, the United States embodied Thomas Jefferson's ideal of an "empire of liberty" (Foner, 2011).

XIV

Examining the Association between Religiosity and Attitudes toward the Legalization of Same-Sex Marriage

The purpose of this research survey was to investigate the association between religiosity and attitudes regarding same-sex marriage in the United States. Specifically, it compared one component of respondents' subjective religiosity, importance of religion, to their support for or against the legalization of gay marriage. Therein, the independent ordinal variable was subjective religiosity, which is conceptually defined as the degree of importance that one places on religion in his or her life. Subjective religiosity is comprised of three fundamental aspects; importance of religion, frequency of prayer, and "born again" status (Smith, Faris, Denton, & Regnerus, 2003).

This study will solely measure importance of religion in order to determine how this aspect of religiosity influences relevant political decisions. The dependent ordinal variable being measured, support for same-sex marriage, represents the respondents' attitudes toward gay marriage (Brumbaugh, Sanchez, Nock, & Wright, 2008). Indicators of this variable will measure attitudes toward homosexuality. Specifically, they will examine the permissiveness of attitudes regarding policies which promote same-sex marriage.

I hypothesized that subjective religiosity would have an inverse relationship with support for same-sex marriage. Accordingly, I expected that those respondents who indicated higher levels of religiosity would convey attitudes comparably less permissive of homosexuality and of gay marriage legalization specifically. Consequently, I anticipated that respondents who indicate lower levels of religiosity would be more supportive of the legalization of same-sex marriage. The survey consisted of a simple 7-item questionnaire of closed- and open-ended questions, which is provided in Appendix A at the end of this chapter.

Sampling Design

I utilized the non-probability convenience sampling method of reliance on available subjects. The study population was comprised of my relatives, friends/acquaintances, and co-workers. Ergo, the sampling frame therein was my personal contacts list. This conscious sampling bias prevented the respondent pool from being truly representative of any larger population. However, given the limited scope of this study, my method may be regarded as purposive, as a means to pretest the questionnaire. Respondents were residents of two states wherein same-sex marriage is not currently permitted by law; New Mexico and Kentucky. The frequency counts (distribution) for the socio-demographic characteristics of the study population are provided in Table 1. The intended study population for a larger research initiative would be residents of states wherein same-sex marriage is not legally recognized.

Table 1. Socio-Demographic Distribution

Gender	#	%	Age	#	%	Education	#	%
Male	3	75%	18-25	3	75%	Some College	3	75%
Female	1	25%	26-35	1	25%	Under-graduate Degree	1	25%
Total	4	100%	Total	4	100%	Total	4	100%

This survey was constructed with the intent of being administered via face-to-face or telephonic interview. I intentionally structured the questionnaire so that respondents would not be able to perceive the precise direction of the questions. This was done in an attempt to mediate the potential for respondents' previous answers to influence their future responses. Accordingly, I interviewed three of the respondents in person and one via telephone. Prior to the start of the interview, I explained that the survey pertained to religious beliefs and political decisions. Respondents were informed that participation was strictly voluntary and that they could end the interview at any time. No respondent requested to terminate the study and the resultant response rate was 100 percent.

Results

Based upon simple counts of the survey responses, I established coding criteria for the open-ended indicator questions. I coded Q3 according to three separate categories; (1) no moral implications, (2) moral/immoral dichotomy (i.e. Heaven/Hell), and (3) moral/immoral dichotomy with a singular religious requirement. Therein, responses were categorized based upon their mention of ethical behavior during one's mortal existence as a determinant of a particular version of the afterlife. Moreover, the third category included responses which specifically mentioned the acceptance of a particular God or prophet.

Similarly, I coded Q7 according to three categories depending upon the respondents' indicated level of support for same-sex marriage legalization; (1) would vote or speak out against, (2) would not vote or speak out either way, and (3) would vote or speak out in favor of. All closed-ended questions (Q1-2 & 4-6) were coded on a 5-point scale through item reversals (e.g. Strongly Agree = 5; Strongly Disagree = 1). Utilizing these data, I compiled scale totals for the independent variable, religiosity, and dependent variable, support for same-sex marriage. The religiosity scale had a potential high of 18 and low of 4, while the support for same-sex marriage scale had a possible high of 13 and low of 3; response item values covered this entire range. The transformed scale items and totals for each respondent are illustrated in Table 2.

Table 2. Individual Scale Items and Totals

Respond ent	Q 1	Q 2	Q 3	Q 4	Q 5	Q 6	Q 7	Religios ity (#/18)	Supp ort (#/13)
R001	1	1	1	1	5	5	3	4	13
R002	3	3	1	1	5	5	3	8	13
R003	4	3	2	2	2	1	2	11	5
R004	5	5	3	5	1	1	1	18	3

In order to test my hypothesis, I determined the correlation value between religiosity (x) and support for same-sex marriage (y) utilizing a correlation co-efficient calculator. When rounded to the nearest thousandth, the results affirmed a correlation of -0.896, which indicated a negative correlation between the two variables. To test the significance level of this correlation, I conducted a two-tailed t-test using the common significance level of alpha=0.05. Since N=4 in this study and degrees of freedom (df)=N-2, the df herein was 2. With these values, the critical value of the correlation was 0.950 (Siegle, 2012). Therefore, the relationship between the two variables in this study did not approach statistical significance. However, the data indicate that a survey of a larger study population may reveal a statistically significant negative correlation between religiosity and support for same-sex marriage.

The most identifiable trend in the data results is evident in the scale totals for respondents 1 and 4. These item values represented both of the most extreme possible negative correlations permitted by the design of the questionnaire. However, this may also indicate that the survey did not allow for the necessary amount of data collection considering that the maximum possible scale totals were realized five separate times. Nonetheless, there was no combination of responses within this survey which refuted my hypothesis. In every instance, higher levels of religiosity corresponded to comparably lower levels of support for same-sex marriage and vice versa. Moreover, even a moderate level of religiosity correlated to less support for same-sex marriage; as indicated by the item values of respondent 3. Therefore, the negative correlation was evident even when responses did not reach the extreme value of either scale total.

Relevance

Wilkinson & Roys (2005) conducted two studies which examined heterosexuals' impressions of gay men and lesbians based upon their exposure to vignettes which described the sexual histories of various targets. These vignettes were restricted to three distinct indicators of sexual orientation; emotion, behaviors, or fantasies. One study included only male targets, while the other included only female targets. The researchers predicted that heterosexual participants who read a vignette describing the sexual behavior of a gay man or lesbian would be more likely to rate the target negatively compared to ratings given by participants who read a fantasy or emotions vignette. They also predicted that impressions of the gay male targets within the behavioral context would be influenced by the respondents' religiosity. However, they applied this secondary hypothesis tentatively in the second study concerning impressions of lesbians due to conservative Christianity's comparable indifference toward gay women.

The populations for Wilkinson and Roys' (2005) studies respectively consisted of 171 and 134 heterosexual undergraduate students from a Midwestern public university who participated for partial completion of a course requirement. Respondents read four vignettes; three with heterosexual targets from each of the components of sexual orientation and one with a homosexual target with a randomly assigned component condition. After reading each vignette, participants indicated their overall impressions of the target according to a 100-point numerical thermometer scale with corresponding verbal anchors. Subsequently, respondents' religiosity was measured via a 13-item Spiritual Support subscale derived from the Spiritual Experience Index-Revised (SEI-R) which utilized a 5-point Likert-type scale.

Results of the first study affirmed that heterosexuals were more likely to rate a homosexual male target in the behavioral context negatively than participants who read a fantasy or emotions vignette. Moreover, there was a negative correlation between respondents' religiosity scores and ratings of male targets in the behavioral context. Importantly, the effect of religiosity on impressions of homosexuals was related to the sexual orientation of the target and not based upon an evaluation of the actual behavior. The findings of the second study also affirmed the primary hypothesis, as participants who read vignettes of lesbians in the behavioral context rated the targets comparably more negatively. Therein, the secondary hypothesis was not upheld as impressions of lesbian targets in all three sexual orientation component conditions became more negative as participants' religiosity scores increased. This indicates that the actual component of sexual orientation may be irrelevant concerning the influence of religiosity on impressions of lesbian targets and that these impressions may be more generalized concerning gay women (Wilkinson & Roys, 2005).

The methods utilized by Wilkinson and Roys (2005) were more specific and focused than my questionnaire, since they isolated the various components of sexual orientation. Accordingly, respondents to my questionnaire were asked about homosexuality in a more abstract way, while those who read the sexual orientation condition vignettes specifically rated a single target. Moreover, their use of the SEI-R provided a more valid measure of religiosity. In my survey study, the SEI-R would have established the independent variable in more concrete operational terms. The researchers' findings affirmed the correlation that was revealed in my study. Their data indicate that the results of my survey may have reached statistical significance if an adequately large study population was employed. Ergo, this study is quite encouraging as it buttresses the case for a large-scale version of my survey, if properly revised.

Discussion and Recommendations for Future Research

The purpose of this study was to examine the correlation between one component of subjective religiosity and support for the legalization of same-sex marriage among residents of U.S. states wherein such marriages are not legally permitted. Therein, I conducted interviews of a homogenous study population according to a survey questionnaire which consisted of indicators of these variables. The results indicated that there may be a negative correlation between subjective religiosity and support for same-sex marriage legalization.

The resultant data revealed a substantial correlation, though it did not reach statistical significance. Therein, the relationships between item values adhered to the hypothesis without notable deviation. Moreover, the responses to indicators within scales did not diverge from expectation. Though the study population was small and selected through non-probability sampling, its homogenous nature mediated the potential influence of socio-demographic characteristics among respondents. Due to their aforementioned relationship with the interviewer, the study population was not a typical representation of a larger populous.

Given the sampling method and frame, the population was predominately familiar with sects of the Christian religion and confined to two U.S. states. There was also an over-representation of individuals from younger age demographics who had received formal post-secondary education. Though the correlation between the two variables did not reach statistical significance, the results of this survey convey that this relationship may provide a useful topic for future research. A subsequent study of adequate scope should survey a heterogeneous population of residents from states which do not legally permit same-sex marriage.

It may be advantageous to include more invasive questions relevant to religious beliefs and acceptance of homosexuality in a larger study. In such a case, the research may benefit from being able to guarantee anonymity via a web-based survey, which would require a reconstruction of the questionnaire. Inclusion of questions which measure social distancing is also advisable. For example, a scaled matrix could be used to measure how accepting respondents would be of a homosexual relative, friend, neighbor, Congressman, etc. During the interviews, respondents did not require clarification on any of the items, which indicates that the current questions were not confusing and may be implemented in a future web-based or mail-in survey.

Before we begin, we would like to collect some demographic information. We will not ask any specific identifying questions, so there will be no way to connect any individual with his or her responses.

Circle the one answer that best applies to you:

What is your gender?

     a.   Male
     b.   Female

What is your age?

     a.   18-25
     b.   26-35
     c.   36-45
     d.   46-60
     e.   61 or over

What is the highest level of education you have completed?

     a.   Less than High School
     b.   High School Diploma / GED
     c.   Some College
     d.   Undergraduate Degree (AA, BA)
     e.   Graduate / Professional Degree (MA, PhD)

In this section, we would like to know a little about your religious beliefs so we can see how different types of people feel about the issues that we will be examining.

Circle the one answer that best applies to you:

1. Which of the following best describes your religious beliefs?

   a. I believe in a personal God
   b. I usually believe in a personal God, but sometimes have doubts
   c. I do not believe in a personal God, but believe there is some kind of Higher Power
   d. I am not sure if I believe in either a God or Higher Power
   e. I do not believe that there is a God or Higher Power

2. How important is religious faith in your life?

   1. Very Important
   2. Important
   3. Neutral
   4. Unimportant
   5. Very Unimportant

3. Do you believe there is an afterlife of any kind (Heaven, Purgatory, Reincarnation, etc.)?

   a. Yes
   b. No

   If you answered yes, please explain…

   _____

   _____

Finally, we would like to know how people feel about the moral and legal issues that are being discussed in the United States today.

<u>Indicate whether you agree or disagree with the following statements by circling the one best answer:</u>

4. Religious leaders should try to influence government decisions.

    a.   Strongly Agree
    b.   Agree
    c.   Neither Agree nor Disagree
    d.   Disagree
    e.   Strongly Disagree

5. It is morally acceptable for two adults of the <u>same</u> gender to have sexual relations.

    a.   Strongly Agree
    b.   Agree
    c.   Neither Agree nor Disagree
    d.   Disagree
    e.   Strongly Disagree

6. Two adults of the <u>same</u> gender should be allowed to legally marry.

    a.   Strongly Agree
    b.   Agree
    c.   Neither Agree nor Disagree
    d.   Disagree
    e.   Strongly Disagree

7. Would you favor, oppose, or neither favor nor oppose a law allowing same-sex couples to legally marry in your state? Please explain your answer...

    _____

    _____

XV

The Influence of Conservative Christianity on the American Public Education System

As the most prevalent faith among the citizenry, Christianity is an omnipresent social institution within American society. However, its survival hinges upon its ability to "...meet the needs of the new day" (Ashworth, 1920). For much of our nation's history, certainly in the wake of the McCarthy Era, it was uncontroversial for schoolchildren to rise every morning and pledge their allegiance to "one nation under God." In fact, parents have been fined an even imprisoned for their children's refusal to recite this nationalistic god-fearing oath (Ryan, 2005).

Today, the debate continues regarding the place for evolution and creationism in public schools. Moreover, the influence of religion on contemporary sexual education programs is axiomatic. Only the protections provided by the Free Exercise and Establishment Clauses of the U.S. Constitution have quelled the comprehensive seepage of Judeo-Christian morality into American culture (Brudney, 2005). Nevertheless, contemporary Christianity continues to influence the education of young Americans in a manner which is likely to reverberate for generations in the arenas of public health and general scientific inquiry. Herein, I examine the issue through the lens of structural functionalism and postulate how two of sociology's revered functionalists would view and potentially remedy the current state of affairs.

The Functionalist Perspective

Structural functionalism holds as a fundamental maxim the fiduciary relationship between social structures which perform positive functions for one another. Ultimately, the viewpoint postulates that social patterns preserve and buttress a larger system; which is indicative of a perpetual equilibrium. Essentially, the functionalist perspective advocates the status quo since the best social change therein is no change (Ritzer, 2011, p. 60). In lieu of revolutionary change, functionalism dictates that parts of societies merely adapt to recapture lost social order. Nonetheless, structural functionalism has been historically criticized for its inability to encompass social change and conflict (Demerath, 1996).

To illustrate a quid pro quo example of the functionalist viewpoint, the State provides public education to children whose families pay taxes which the State requires in hopes that the children will mature to become law-abiding taxpayers; a cyclic exchange of money for the assurance of a quality education. However, in the event of a recession, governmental programs are often cut and families are forced to regulate their budgets in an attempt to regain the former stability.

Consequently, religion may be a mechanism employed to maintain order within the public school system through the indoctrination of nationalism and morality. Perhaps, this is done in order to ensure that schoolchildren do, in fact, grow up to become productive members of society with a firm understanding of social norms and expectations. Accordingly, the actual recitation of the Pledge of Allegiance may be viewed as a manifest function, with the development of patriotism and establishment of a moral code constituting the latent functions of the ceremony.

Talcott Parsons on the Religious Sector and Educational Sphere

Talcott Parsons revolutionized sociological theory with the publication of *The Structure of Social Action.* Ultimately, he contributed significantly to the rise of structural functionalism in American sociology (Ritzer, 2011, pp. 54-56). Though generally concerned with macro-level analyses, Parsons spent much of his time investigating the progressive differentiation of religions and shifts in the educational sphere (Martin, 1979).

A running theme in Parson's understanding of social change theory was the formation of Western society through the Protestant notion of universal salvation. He held that universal values were vital to the process of modernization, but contended that universalistic norms could not develop in a functioning society without social differentiation. Parson's view of social change necessitated the growth of individual freedoms and an abstract concept of social membership unencumbered by identifiers such as race and gender (Turner, 1993). Perhaps, one may postulate that creed could be added to a more modern variation of Parson's social membership criteria.

Importantly, Parsons realized the negative consequences of isolating the nuclear family from a wider kinship group; something which conservative and fundamentalist Christianity often encourage. In advanced societies such as the United States, contradictory demands on the mother, particularly with the rise in prevalence of single-parent households and increasing female employment, deepen social strain and pose problems for Parson's somewhat antiquated view of the family (Turner, 1993).

In my opinion, Parsons would likely support the current role of religion in public education as a means of establishing universal values. However, this notion would become exceedingly difficult to implement within an increasingly diversified secular society and may even degrade social membership. Moreover, he may advocate a removal, or at least revision, of all government-sponsored sexual education programs from middle- and secondary-school curricula, effectively placing the burden on the now dying nuclear family. Although, church-based sexuality education programs may provide a viable alternative to holders of the Parsonian perspective as they have been shown to be relatively effective at raising self-esteem and clarifying personal sexual values (Powell & Jorgensen, 1985). Moreover, this approach would be in agreement with Parson's appreciation of Puritanical values, albeit potentially outdated.

Robert Merton: Puritanism and Science

Robert Merton was Parson's most famous pupil and became the first sociologist to be admitted to the National Academy of Sciences (Cole, 2004; Ritzer, 2011, pp. 54-55). Notably, the subject of his 1938 doctoral dissertation was Puritanism and science (Cole, 2004). As noted by Nelkin (2004), controversy surrounds the alleged religious and moral implications of science. Young-Earth Creationists have vehemently opposed the assimilation of evolutionary biology into public school curricula; robbing young Americans of an adequate education in the physical and life sciences. Additionally, the purported implications of "social" Darwinism are often misrepresented and exaggerated in political discourse and media (Orr, 2009). However, limiting children's exposure to scientific theory certainly serves the aforementioned social function of facilitating the institution of morality and upholding the subjective values of a patriarchal society under God the Father by instilling a respect for masculine authority.

Importantly, as a graduate student, Merton devoted much of his time to the measurement of rates of progress in Arabian intellectual history, of which religion played a significant role. Ultimately, he concluded in his dissertation that science flourishes in societies wherein scientific activity is highly regarded (Cole, 2004). Therefore, I believe that Merton would view the current influence of religion within the American public education system as a refusal to accept positivism and a potential threat to the technological and intellectual advancement of American society.

So long as biblical literalism influences education, progress in the fields of science and technology will be lackluster and piecemeal; much in the same way that the prior Catholic hegemony, unlike Protestantism, discouraged scientific inquiry in 17th Century England. Moreover, Merton elaborated on what he termed the "foci of attention" and demonstrated that scientists were primarily influenced by the practical concerns of the day (Cole, 2004). Therefore, it occurs to me that he would encourage the teaching of evolution in public schools if only to mediate the influence of Christianity and empower American youths with the necessary knowledge to make a significant future impact on scientific inquiry and experimentation; particularly in genetic, molecular, and conservation biology.

Conclusion and Reflection

Through the functionalist viewpoint, it is difficult to gain a comprehensive understanding of the influence of Christian values on the American public education system, largely due to its penchant for ignoring conflict and instead focusing on the positive functions performed by associated social structures. The relationship between religiously-supported nationalism and the indoctrination of social values appears to instill a Judeo-Christian sense of morality in young Americans. However, collaterally, it negatively impacts the quality of science education in public schools and poses legitimate public health concerns for adolescents and teens. Perhaps, this is illustrative of equilibrium between the institutions of religion and education. However, if evolution is discarded while faith-inspired abstinence-only sexual education programs are continually incorporated into school curricula, these structures may need to adapt in order to regain stability.

XVI

Identifying Firearm Availability as a Risk Factor for Homicide Victimization and Suicide

Gun control is a topic of considerable debate in American discourse; one inextricably linked to political and ideological beliefs that have roots traceable to the nation's founding. Consequently, research concerning access to firearms and rates of intentional death has been purported to substantiate either a significant association or non-relationship, often depending upon the affiliation of the interpreting body. Regardless, the evidence suggests quite clearly that, largely independent of environmental and socio-cultural factors, firearm availability shares a considerable positive correlation with the risk of homicide victimization and suicide (Morgenstern, 1997).

Indeed, firearms have the potential to make interpersonal encounters more volatile than they may have been otherwise and greater access to firearms increases the chance that a gun will be used in an attack; making it more likely that any given assault will result in the victim's death (Zimring, 1968). Moreover, the availability of a firearm makes the facilitation of suicide more accessible, permitting an individual to make a permanent decision on impulse without the forethought generally inherent to more traditional methods (Ajdacic-Gross et al., 2008). Identifying the association between firearm availability and overall rates of intentional death is necessary so that viable options may be adopted which can mediate this risk through cogent gun law reform.

The Second Amendment of the U.S. Constitution, one of the few elements of the Bill of Rights that has not been selectively incorporated, provides that "...the right of the people to keep and bear arms, shall not be infringed." However, while the Supreme Court affirmed the individual right to keep suitable firearms for lawful purposes in *District of Columbia v. Heller*, it has also upheld federal attempts to regulate specific weapons as well as the authority of states and municipalities to implement gun control legislation. The Court has historically and consistently held that the right to keep and bear arms is subject to regulation (Library of Congress, 2012).

Nevertheless, of the 178 countries surveyed by the Geneva-based Graduate Institute of International and Development Studies (2011), the United States maintains by far the highest national per-capita rate of privately-owned small arms; boasting nearly double the firearm density of Switzerland and 10 times that of Russia. American citizens represent less than five percent of the global population, yet own nearly one-third of all the world's approximated 870 million registered firearms. Take a moment to appreciate that statistic. To put these data in perspective, researchers were able to account for approximately 88.8 privately-owned firearms for every 100 people in the United States. Annually, about half of the 36,900 suicides and nearly 70 percent of the 16,800 homicides committed in the U.S. are perpetrated with firearms (Centers for Disease Control and Prevention, 2011). Accordingly, the need to investigate any relationship that firearm availability may have with rates of homicide victimization and suicide is axiomatic.

Cross-National Trends in Firearm-Related Homicide

Among developed nations, the United States is the undisputed leader in homicide. Interestingly, the level of overall crime in America is not demonstrably different from that of comparable countries, though the preponderance of lethal violence in the U.S. is much greater; four times higher than the average for other industrialized nations (Zimring & Hawkins, 1997). Notably, the national prevalence of violence is independent of poverty as the majority of developing countries report lower homicide rates than the U.S. as well. Though still a hot topic of contention among Americans, most foreign criminologists identify firearm availability as the single best explanation for the United States' epidemic of lethal violence, since roughly half of Americans reportedly own at least one firearm; which is three times the per-capita firearm density of most other high-income nations (Hoskin, 2001).

A review of the extant literature conducted by Hepburn and Hemenway (2004) revealed that the availability of firearms is a risk factor for homicide in high-income countries. Throughout developed nations with greater access to guns, residents are at a higher risk of homicide and there appears to be no quantifiable benefit to firearm ownership regarding the number of lives potentially saved by firearms used in self-defense. Importantly, this association holds true for developed nations even when the United States is excluded. There is insufficient data to claim direct causation, but the preponderance of evidence suggests that firearm availability shares a positive relationship with the risk of homicide victimization in high-income countries, apparently independent of environmental and socio-cultural factors.

Though the United States is unique in terms of the sheer proliferation of firearms in civilian possession, case studies conducted in other developed nations convey that the strict regulation of certain types of firearms may reduce homicide victimization and mass fatal spree shootings; which are a seemingly omnipresent media talking point in America. Chapman, Alpers, Agho, and Jones (2006) undertook a program evaluation of the sweeping gun law reforms put in place to remove various semi-automatic weapons and pump-action shotguns from civilian possession by the Australian government in the aftermath of a 1996 massacre in Tasmania wherein 35 civilians were killed by a lone gunman. They assessed trends in total firearm deaths, instances of mass fatal shootings, as well as rates of both firearm-related and total homicides from 18 years prior to the reforms to 10.5 years after.

The results of the study affirmed that the declines in total firearm-related deaths and firearm homicides that had preceded the reforms appeared to have accelerated significantly immediately following their implementation. Moreover, there was no observed substitution effect of other methods being employed in overall homicide rates; which illustrates the lethality of a firearm compared to any other common medium of interpersonal violence. Notably, while there had been 13 mass fatal shootings in Australia in the 18 years before the reforms, when gun laws had been relatively lenient, none had occurred in the subsequent decade. However, such spree shootings are rare, isolated, and nuanced by myriad individual factors. Therefore, these data, impressive as they are, should not be over-generalized. Nonetheless, this study affirmed that appropriately targeted gun control legislation can decrease citizens' risk of homicide victimization; conveying a direct association between firearm availability and overall national homicide rates.

Hoskin (2001) completed one of the most extensive and oft-repeated cross-national comparative analyses of firearm availability and homicide rates, which examined this association across 36 countries. Using an established survey-based measure of firearm availability and a national homicide rate averaged over multiple years, the results affirmed a statistically significant positive relationship between firearm availability and national homicide rates. As guns become more accessible, the likelihood that a perpetrator will use a firearm in the commission of a crime increases. Subsequently, there is a proportionally heightened risk that the victim will die from injuries sustained during a given attack.

It is also noteworthy that the firearm in and of itself may embolden a criminal who would otherwise not be able physically and/or psychologically to inflict fatal damage. Accordingly, lethal violence is likely to be more prevalent in countries that have greater access to privately-owned firearms. The data also suggest that homicide rates are higher in nations that are ethnically heterogeneous and in those which maintain conservative welfare programs. Consequently, observations made in the United States fit these projections. It has an ethnically diverse population, allocates relatively little money toward social programs compared to other developed nations, and leads the world in private firearm possession. Importantly, the firearm availability association holds true even when these additional social factors are controlled; though they also contribute to national homicide rates.

Firearm Density and Homicide Victimization in the United States

The prevalence of firearms in American society is so significant that it impacts every single resident to some degree. In fact, gun violence shortens the average American's life by 104 days. Notably, the effect is particularly pronounced among men; 151 days for Caucasian and nearly one full year for African-American males. Of all fatal injuries, only motor vehicle accidents have a more significant impact on life expectancies in the U.S. The effect is so significant that it must be accounted for in medical insurance premiums across the nation (Lemaire, 2005). Regardless, the fact that gender, race, and socio-economic characteristics influence the association does not mediate the significance of the relationship between firearms density and risk of homicide. Within the United States, firearm availability is inextricably linked to homicide victimization rates at the regional, state, and municipal levels.

Though the vast majority of American homicide victims are killed with firearms, critics often contend that this phenomenon is unrelated to household firearm ownership, arguing that legally owned weapons should not pose any threat to public safety. Accordingly, Miller, Azrael, and Hemenway (2002c) utilized cross-sectional time-series data to investigate the association between homicide rates and household firearm ownership at the regional and state levels over a 10-year period. Though unable to definitively determine causation, the study revealed that a disproportionate number of people died via homicide in areas with higher rates of household firearm ownership.

Regionally, the association was noticeably pronounced for victims aged 5 to 14 years and for those 35 years and older, though it did not reach statistical significance for other age groups. The findings also revealed that non-gun homicides were slightly elevated in these areas and that rates of household handgun ownership were more likely to be associated than simple measures of household ownership of all firearms; indicating that available methods may indeed perpetuate a culture of violence. Ergo, firearm density may contribute to higher levels of violence in other forms as well.

The results of the state-level analysis were even more significant. Therein, after controlling for various socio-economic factors, the data affirmed a positive association between household firearm ownership and homicide rates among all persons over age 5 and was especially evident in victims over age 25. As with the regional analysis, the primary contributor to the elevated homicide rates was the prevalence of firearm-related homicide in states with higher rates of household firearm ownership. Ultimately, a person over age 5 living in a "high gun state" was more than 2.5 times more likely to become a homicide victim than a comparable person living in a "low gun state" for no other observable reason than firearm availability (Miller, Azrael, and Hemenway, 2002c).

The authors later examined survey-based estimates of household firearm ownership and homicide mortality over a three-year period in order to more narrowly examine the role that household firearms played in homicide victimization at the state level; since firearm ownership rates vary much less within states than between states and across regions. Ultimately, they reaffirmed that states with higher levels of household firearm ownership displayed significantly higher rates of homicide victimization across their respective populations (Miller, Hemenway, & Azrael, 2007). Therefore, greater levels of household firearm ownership corresponded to an increased risk of firearm-related death and a subsequently higher overall homicide rate.

The association between firearm availability and homicide rates holds true even in micro-level studies. In fact, it appears that the relationship becomes even more significant as the methodology becomes more focused.

McDowall (1991) investigated the trend solely within the confines of the city limits of Detroit, Michigan over a 35-year period. Importantly, the author did not rely on standard self-report measures of firearm availability, but instead calculated firearm density based upon the relative frequency with which guns were utilized in the commission of robberies and suicides; which allows for greater validity. The results confirmed that higher levels of firearm density corresponded to an increased risk of homicide in the city. The model showed that for every 1 percent increase in gun density, the rate of homicides per 100,000 inhabitants rose slightly more than 1 percent.

Although, Detroit's excessively high murder rates cannot be solely attributed to firearm density; there are certainly myriad social and economic factors to consider as well. More importantly, the results revealed an association that is generally overlooked in broader analyses; that homicide rates should fall if firearm density could be reduced. Interestingly, the data conveyed that the demand for firearms may be influenced by the prevalence of violent crime in a given area; constituting a self-perpetuating arms race fueled by citizens' fear of crime. Consequently, municipal gun control regulations may be the least desired and least successful where they would actually be the most beneficial.

Firearm Availability and Deterrence

Numerous independent studies using varying methods have affirmed a significant correlation between firearm availability and homicide victimization. However, qualitative arguments have been offered which purportedly substantiate the benefits of firearm ownership for protection. Some commentators have asserted that, through self-defense, household firearm ownership has saved lives that would have otherwise ended in homicide. In this vein, access to firearms is regarded as a general deterrent and life preserver. Nonetheless, at every echelon from cross-national down to municipal, increasing levels of gun availability raise the likelihood that a citizen will become the victim of a homicide, while there is no evidence that greater access to firearms can reduce any category of violent crime.

Moreover, generally less than 300 homicides perpetrated by private citizens in any given year are cleared as "justifiable" in the U.S., about 80 percent of which involve firearms (Federal Bureau of Investigation, 2011). Consequently, by comparison to the national homicide rate, the impact of firearm-related justifiable homicides is infinitesimal. Lott (2000) conducted the most famous of the very few studies which have found that increasing gun availability may have a deterrence effect. However, the results have come under serious scrutiny and been challenged by several prominent criminologists (Altheimer, 2010). A consensus has not yet been reached, but subjective support for firearm access as a deterrent is sparse and hard evidence even more so.

Paradoxically, the same researchers who condemn their opponents for relying on survey-based measures of firearm availability often base their own assertions on self-reports of victimizations that would have supposedly ended in the death of innocents had the attacks not been thwarted with a firearm. Kleck (1997) argued that increasing gun availability can reduce crime through the empowerment of would-be victims. Purportedly, an armed victim may prevent a crime by neutralizing an aggressor and shifting the balance of power or by resisting an offender to avoid injury. The resultant, and purely theoretical, deterrence effect would reduce crime by making attackers fearful of potentially armed victims. Regardless, the data simply does not support these contentions. There is no evidence which suggests a negative association between firearm availability and violent crime rates.

In discussions of constitutional rights and self-defense, firearm proficiency is all too often ignored. Numerous studies have shown that active duty police officers, with extensive training in marksmanship and gun-handling, display abysmal accuracy in field shooting scenarios; by comparison to controlled range firing. When engaging live assailants which, unlike paper targets, pose a physical threat, officers' incident hit rates are usually less than 30 percent, though sporadic reports of hit rates of 50-60 percent have been reported by individual departments.

Moreover, in incidents involving mutual gunplay, officers are usually struck by assailants' bullets about one-third of the time. Importantly, these data do not mention the actual fatality rate of officer-involved shootings, because the ultimate purpose behind the employment of a weapon for a law enforcement officer is to stop the individual; a fatal wound is not always required (Morrison & Vila, 1998). This raises obvious questions regarding an armed citizens' ability to exercise discretion in such scenarios. Additionally, the risk of injury and death to bystanders cannot be responsibly overlooked. There is also a legitimate argument to be made that the presence of a firearm may compel citizens to become involved in situations that they would otherwise have avoided. Ultimately, access to a gun increases the risk of injury and death to everyone within its effective range.

Not only does firearm ownership increase one's risk of homicide victimization, it provides no tangible benefit relative to self-defense or the preservation of life (Hepburn & Hemenway, 2004). Public demand for firearm access only perpetuates this trend. It seems plausible that citizens in areas of high gun crime may feel as though their governors have failed to protect them. Consequently, household firearms become a security blanket that they are unwilling to relinquish even when doing so could facilitate the implementation of efficacious gun reform. The introduction of a firearm into any given encounter serves only to raise the likelihood of death for all parties involved; perpetrator, victim, and bystanders (Hoskin, 2001). Ergo, armed citizens may actually increase the risk of victimization to themselves and everyone around them.

Preferred Methods of Suicide

Unlike homicide which is contingent upon the actions or inactions of at least two individuals, victim and attacker, the decision to take one's own life is comparably more intimate. Ostensibly, there is very little that could be done, certainly at least from a legislative perspective, which could prevent suicides on any quantifiable scale. Nonetheless, the completion of a suicide requires desire, ability, and feasibility. A detached governmental body cannot adequately address desire, but both ability and feasibility are directly impacted by one's access to firearms. Consequently, an ever-growing compendium of research suggests that firearm availability not only increases the risk that a suicide will be attempted, but that any given attempt will result in the loss of life.

In order to investigate potential intervention protocols, Ajdacic-Gross et al. (2008) conducted the first international study of preferred suicide methods utilizing data collected from the World Health Organization's mortality database. The authors determined that poisoning by pesticides and drugs were the most popular methods in Latin America and Asia, while firearm suicide was most common in the United States. These comparably more technical methods do not require as much forethought and planning as traditional methods such as hanging and become increasingly popular as countries develop. Most importantly, the preferred suicide method of any country depends largely upon its availability.

In developed nations, access to technical means of suicide is of significant importance. Particularly, firearm-related suicides depend more on the availability of the method than do other forms. Accordingly, Ajdacic-Gross et al. (2006) examined fluctuations in the suicide rates of several Western nations relative to changes in household firearm ownership. In their longitudinal study, the authors identified several countries that displayed obvious declines in overall suicide rates. Private firearm ownership was inextricably linked to this trend as gun access is a well-established risk factor for suicide. In each case, the proportion of firearm-related suicides and private firearm ownership decreased simultaneously and proportionally.

In most countries with declining suicide rates, firearm registration and relevant legislation had become progressively more restrictive. With only two exceptions, Canada and Australia, overall suicide rates declined along with firearm suicides; indicating that there was no substitution effect of other methods employed to compensate. Accordingly, it is reasonable to speculate that a large number of suicides would not have been attempted and certainly less completed if a firearm had not been available at the time. This further substantiates the importance of access to methods of suicide and alludes to the comparably greater lethality of firearms.

Household Firearm Ownership and Risk of Suicide

Firearms are the most commonly employed method of suicide across all demographics in the United States (Brent & Bridge, 2003). In fact, more Americans commit suicide with firearms than with all other methods combined. Miller, Azrael, and Hemenway (2002b) examined whether the disproportionate employment of firearms as a means of suicide had any impact on overall suicide rates, or if it merely represented a reallocation of methods. Using regional and state-level data covering a 10-year period, the authors analyzed levels of household firearm ownership compared to rates of overall suicide, firearm-specific suicide, and non-firearm suicide. The results affirmed that for the entire U.S. population, regardless of gender and for virtually every age group, household firearm ownership was positively associated with all suicide rates. Simply put, a disproportionate number of residents die from suicide, not just firearm-related, in areas with higher levels of firearm ownership.

To investigate this association further, Miller, Lippmann, Azrael, and Hemenway (2007) included survey-based estimates of serious mental illness and substance abuse to control for psychological risk factors. The results confirmed that, independent of demographic and socio-economic characteristics, Americans are more likely to commit suicide when they reside in an area with a higher prevalence of privately-owned firearms. As expected, rates of non-firearm suicide did not appear to be associated with firearm access. Ergo, having access to a firearm increases the chance that an individual, who otherwise would not consider suicide by different means, will attempt and complete a suicide.

While the evidence in support of the positive association between firearm availability and risk of suicide is substantial, the existence of such a relationship also dictates that decreasing levels of firearm access should contribute to lower suicide rates. Accordingly, Miller, Azrael, Hepburn, Hemenway, and Lippmann (2006) studied declines in household firearm ownership across all four regions of the U.S. over a 22-year period to assess whether or not they were associated with changes in suicide rates. The data indicated that each 10 percent reduction in household firearm ownership contributed to declines of 4.2 percent in firearm suicides and 2.5 percent in overall suicides.

Nonetheless, the most significant relationships were discovered among the 0-19 age demographic. Therein, each 10 percent decline in households with both firearms and children was associated with reductions of 8.3 percent in firearm suicides and 4.1 in overall suicides. As affirmed in previous studies, no association was found between firearm ownership and rates of non-firearm suicide, which suggests the absence of any quantifiable substitution effect. Ergo, reducing access to firearms in private homes has the potential to preserve lives, especially those of American children and teen-agers that may otherwise have ended on impulse.

Suicide and American Youth

Firearms are the 3rd leading cause of death for American children and teen-agers; superseded only by motor vehicle accidents and cancer. The elevated rates of homicide, suicide and accidental death among 5-14 year-olds is not explainable by socio-economic factors such as poverty and urbanization, but driven by lethal firearm violence (Miller, Azrael, & Hemenway, 2002a). Not surprisingly, the U.S. suffers the highest national rate of firearm suicide in the industrialized world; 11 times that of the average for other developed nations among children under age 15. For over two decades ending in the late 1990s, the firearm-related suicide rate among 15 to 19 year-olds rose twice as fast as the rate of suicide by all other means combined. Consequently, the noticeable rise in overall suicide rates among American youths since 1960 is primarily attributable to the increase in firearm-related suicides (Brent & Bridge, 2003).

A compendium of studies has confirmed that youths are disproportionately affected by the impact of firearm availability. Using data from the nine census regions of the U.S. from 1979-94, Birckmayer & Hemenway (2001) concluded that firearm ownership levels were correlated with suicide rates among Americans younger than 25. During the time period studied, regional rates of overall suicide and firearm-related suicide remained relatively stable, though the percentage of suicides committed with a guns increased among 15-24 year-olds. For this age group, overall suicide rates were found to be positively associated with firearm availability. Though ecological studies using survey-based measures are inadequate to definitively establish statistical causation, the findings suggested that a 10 percent decline in regional firearm ownership would prompt reductions of 3 percent in overall suicide and 8.2 percent in firearm-related suicide. Ergo, the availability of a lethal instrument is a major determinant in completed suicide among all age groups, but disproportionately affects Americans under 25 who are arguably more impetuous.

Firearm suicides are unique as they are more often the result of impulsive decisions than is found to be the case with traditional means. For instance, when compared to victims of other suicide methods, those who employed firearms generally have a history of significantly fewer suicide attempts. This is indicative of the obvious fact that, no matter the degree of desire, methods of lower lethality are less likely to result in the completion of a suicide attempt.

Previous research has also shown that suicidal individuals are more likely to abandon their attempts when presented with obstacles, such as a more elaborate traditional method. Indeed, tying a noose, cutting one's wrists in a bath tub or driving out to a point of sufficient elevation all require a certain amount of deliberate forethought and planning. More importantly, the added steps required to complete these tasks pose physical and chronological obstacles. In this regard, reducing firearm availability would be tantamount to the detoxification of household gasses, reduced sizing of drug packages, and the heightened security / increased patrolling of bridges; all of which have been proven successful at preventing suicide attempts (Ajdacic-Gross et al., 2006). Like previously-employed prevention methods, reducing access to firearms has the potential to save American lives, particularly among children, that may have otherwise ended prematurely.

Conclusion and Discussion

Numerous studies have investigated the relationship between firearm availability and rates of both homicide and suicide at every jurisdictional level. The evidence in support of a positive association has been consistent throughout. Nonetheless, to many, the collective findings remain ambiguous and unconvincing. The primary reason for this lack of acceptance has been the questionable validity of survey-based measures of household gun ownership. For instance, some studies have found that measures used in much of the extant research were of poor validity due to the inherently subjective nature of self-reports. However, the results of these analyses also suggest that there are no known measures of firearm availability that would be conducive to a credible longitudinal study of its association with homicide rates (Kleck, 2004). As much as one may debate that this is little more than an excuse not to address the root of a very serious problem, it would be disingenuous to ignore the distinction between a positive association and a causal relationship; the former being all that has truly been substantiated at this point. Nonetheless, the preponderance of evidence is certainly making it ever more plausible that access to firearms has a direct influence on homicide victimization.

Regardless of the accusations of statistical manipulation and over-generalization, even many who contend that no relationship has been established agree that the most cogent measure of firearm availability is the percentage of suicides committed with firearms (Kleck, 2004). Ergo, the fact that about half of all suicides in the United States are firearm-related is indicative of a high national rate of firearm availability (Centers for Disease Control and Prevention, 2011). Such is why McDowall's (1991) findings in Detroit which incorporated this measure were so significant. Moreover, the impact of having access to a gun on the likelihood of completed suicide has been repeatedly substantiated (Miller, Lippmann, Azrael, & Hemenway, 2007). Consequently, it would be nothing short of intellectual treachery to ignore the axiomatic relationship between firearm availability and overall suicide rates; one that is especially pronounced among children. Though merely educated conjecture, it seems reasonable to suspect that firearm access has had a similar influence on homicide rates.

Until an alternative theory is presented which can account for this correlation and also control for socio-economic and cultural characteristics, firearm availability must be regarded as a risk factor for homicide victimization and suicide. One would be hard-pressed to think of another issue that is so obviously important to criminal justice policy in the U.S., yet so often ignored in criminological research and public discourse; except perhaps during times of national mourning. Thousands of Americans will die this year, just as last year, from firearm-related violence, whether interpersonal or self-inflicted. If only after another massacre, analysts will not be able to shirk their responsibility to provide policy makers with unambiguous results free of ideological biases for much longer. Clearly, more empirical research is needed to understand, not only sources of violence in general, but the specific impact that firearms have on homicide and suicide in the United States. Nonetheless, the need for timely and responsible gun law reform is axiomatic.

References

Chapter I:

Aaronson, D. E. (2008). Cross-racial identification of defendants in criminal cases: A proposed model jury instruction. *Criminal Justice, 23*(1), 4-12.

Anderson, J. B. (2005). Hamdi v. Rumsfeld: Judicious balancing at the intersection of the executive's power to detain and the citizen-detainee's right to due process. *Journal of Criminal Law & Criminology, 95*(3), 689-723.

Blackerby, J. C. (2003). Life after death row: Preventing wrongful capital convictions and restoring innocence after exoneration. *Vanderbilt Law Review, 56*(4), 1179-1226.

Bowman, L. E. (2008). Lemonade out of lemons: Can wrongful convictions lead to criminal justice reform? *Journal of Criminal Law & Criminology, 98*(4), 1501-1517.

Campbell, K. & Denov, M. (2004). The burden of innocence: Coping with a wrongful imprisonment1. *Canadian Journal of Criminology and Criminal Justice, 46*(2), 139-163.

Cassell, P. G. (1998). Protecting the innocent from false confessions and lost confessions—and from Miranda. *Journal of Criminal Law & Criminology, 88*(2), 497-556.

Chambliss, W. J. (1973). The saints and the roughnecks. *Society, 11,* 24-31.

Clark, S. E. & Godfrey, R. D. (2009). Eyewitness identification evidence and innocence risk. *Psychonomic Bulletin & Review, 16*(1), 22-42.

Crone, J. A. (2011). *How can we solve our social problems?* (2nd ed.). Los Angeles, CA: Sage.

Cross, F. B. (2005). Law and trust. *Georgetown Law Journal, 93*(5), 1457-1545.

Darabont, F. (Director). (1994). *The shawshank redemption* [Motion picture]. United States: Castle Rock Entertainment.

Darabont, F. (Director). (1999). *The green mile* [Motion picture]. United States: Warner Bros. Pictures.

Garrett, B. L. (2012). Learning from patterns of mistakes. *Criminal Justice, 26*(4), 30-35, 42.

Givelber, D. (2005). Lost innocence: Speculation and data about the acquitted. *The American Criminal Law Review, 42*(4), 1167-1199.

Gould, J. B. (2008). The lessons of wrongful convictions. *Criminal Justice Ethics, 27*(1), 2108-2111.

Gould, J. B. & Leo, R. A. (2010). One hundred years later: Wrongful convictions after a century of research. *Journal of Criminal Law & Criminology, 100*(3), 825-868.

Halsted, J. B. (1992). The anti-drug policies of the 1980s: Have they increased the likelihood of both wrongful convictions and sentencing disparities? *Criminal Justice Policy Review, 6*(3), 207-228.

Harmon, T. R. (2004). Race for your life: An analysis of the role of race in erroneous capital convictions. *Criminal Justice Review, 29*(1), 76-96.

Huff, C. R. (2002). Wrongful conviction and public policy: The American Society of Criminology 2001 Presidential address. *Criminology, 40*(1), 1-18.

Huff, C. R. (2004). Wrongful convictions: The American experience. *Canadian Journal of Criminology and Criminal Justice, 46*(2), 107-120.

Huff, C. R., Rattner, A., Sagarin, E., & MacNamara, D. E. J. (1986). Guilty until proven innocent: Wrongful conviction and public policy. *Crime & Delinquency, 32*(4), 518-544.

Jackiw, L. B., Arbuthnott, K. D., Pfeifer, J. E., Marcon, J. L., & Meissner, C. A. (2008). Examining the cross-race effect in lineup identification using Caucasian and First Nations samples. *Canadian Journal of Behavioural Science, 40*(1), 52-57.

Krieger, S. A. (2011). Why our justice system convicts innocent people, and the challenges faced by innocence projects trying to exonerate them. *New Criminal Law Review, 14*(3), 333-402.

Leo, R. A. & Gould, J. B. (2009). Studying wrongful convictions: Learning from social science. *Ohio State Journal of Criminal Law, 7*(7), 7-30.

Leo, R. A. (2005). Rethinking the study of miscarriages of justice: Developing a criminology of wrongful conviction. *Journal of Contemporary Criminal Justice, 21*(3), 201-223.

Leon-Guerrero, A. (2011). *Social problems: Community, policy, and social action* (3rd ed.). Los Angeles, CA: Sage.

Marquis, J. (2005). The myth of innocence. *Journal of Criminal Law & Criminology, 95*(2), 501-521.

Martin, A. W. (1998). Prosecutorial misconduct. *Georgetown Law Journal, 86*(5), 1677-1693.

Oaksford, M. & Hahn, U. (2004). A Bayesian approach to the argument from ignorance. *Canadian Journal of Experimental Psychology, 58*(2), 75-85.

Ousey, G. C. & Lee, M. R. (2010). To know the unknown: The decline in homicide clearance rates, 1980-2000. *Criminal Justice Review, 35*(2), 141-158.

Rattner, A. (1988). Convicted but innocent: Wrongful conviction and the criminal justice system. *Law and Human Behavior, 12*(3), 283-293.

Rothstein, M. A. & Talbott, M. K. (2006). The expanding use of DNA in law enforcement: What role for privacy? *The Journal of Law, Medicine & Ethics, 34*(2), 153-164.

Risinger, D. M. (2007). Innocents convicted: An empirically justified factual wrongful conviction rate. *Journal of Criminal Law & Criminology, 97*(3), 761-806.

Schmalleger, F. & Smykla, J. O. (2009). *Corrections in the 21st Century* (4th ed.). New York, NY: McGraw Hill.

Siegel, A. M. (2005). Moving down the wedge of injustice: A proposal for a third generation of wrongful convictions scholarship and advocacy. *The American Criminal Law Review, 42*(4), 1219-1237.

Steinback, R. (2007). The fight for post-conviction DNA testing is not yet over: An analysis of the eight remaining "holdout states" and suggestions for strategies to bring vital relief to the wrongfully convicted. *Journal of Criminal Law & Criminology, 98*(1), 329-361.

Taslitz, A. E. (2006). Wrongly accused: Is race a factor in convicting the innocent? *Ohio State Journal of Criminal Law, 4*, 121-133.

U.S. Census Bureau. (2011). *Current population reports: Income, poverty, and health insurance coverage in the United States, 2010.* Washington, DC: U.S. Government Printing Office.

U.S. Department of Justice: Federal Bureau of Investigation. (2011, September). *Crime in the United States, 2010.* Retrieved from   http://www.fbi.gov/about-us/cjis/ucr/crime-in-the-u.s/2010/crime-in-the-u.s.-2010/clearancetopic.pdf

U.S. Department of State. (2011, October). *Background note: Hong   Kong.*   Retrieved   from http://www.state.gov/r/pa/ei/bgn/2747.htm

Weber, N. & Perfect, T. J. (2012). Improving eyewitness identification accuracy by screening out those who say they don't know. *Law and Human Behavior, 36*(1), 28-36.

Zalman, M. (2006). Criminal justice system reform and wrongful conviction: A research agenda. *Criminal Justice Policy Review, 17*(4), 468-492.

Zalman, M., Larson, M. J., & Smith, B. (2012). Citizens' attitudes toward wrongful convictions. *Criminal Justice Review, 37*(1), 51-69.

Chapter II:

Illustrations

Table 1. Walter J. Dickey and Pam Hollenhorst, 1999, "Three-Strikes Laws: Five Years Later," *Corrections Management Quarterly*, 3 (3): 4-7.

Figure 1. Schiraldi, Vincent, Jason Colburn, and Eric Lotke, *Three Strikes and You're Out: An Examination of the Impact of 3-Strikes Laws 10 Years after Their Enactment.* Justice Policy Institute, http://www.justicepolicy.org/uploads/justicepolicy/documents/04-09_rep_threestrikesnatl_ac.pdf.pdf

Figure 2. Tomislav Kovandzic V, John J. Sloan III, and Lynne M. Vieraitis, 2004, "'Striking Out' as Crime Reduction Policy: The Impact of 'Three Strikes' Laws on Crime Rates in U.S. Cities," *Justice Quarterly*, 21 (2): 222.

Figure 3. John F. Pfaff, 2008, "The Empirics of Prison Growth: A Critical Review and Path Forward," *Journal of Criminal Law & Criminology*, 98 (2): 550.

Table 2. Kathleen Auerhahn, 2004, "California's Incarcerated Drug Offender Population, Yesterday, Today, and Tomorrow: Evaluating the War on Drugs and Proposition 36,"*Journal of Drug Issues*, 34 (1): 104.

Figure 4. California Department of Corrections and Rehabilitation, Historical Trends, 1987-2007, 2008, http://www.cdcr.ca.gov/Reports_Research/Offender_Informati on_Services_Branch/Annual/HIST2/HIST2d2007.pdf

Figure 5. Washington Department of Corrections, Major Sentencing Changes Impacting Community Supervision Caseloads and Prison Population, 2012, http://www.doc.wa.gov/aboutdoc/docs/MajorSentencingChan gesImpactingCommunitySupervisionCaseloadsandPrisonPop ulation_001.pdf

Sources

Auerhahn, K. (2004). California's incarcerated drug offender population, yesterday, today, and tomorrow: Evaluating the War on Drugs and Proposition 36. *Journal of Drug Issues, 34*(1), 95-120.

Austin, J., Clark, J., Hardyman, P., & Henry, D. A. (1999). The impact "Three Strikes and You're Out." *Punishment & Society, 1*(2), 131-162.

Berliner, L. (1994). Three strikes and you're out: Will the community be safer? *Journal of Interpersonal Violence, 9*(3), 420-421.

California Department of Corrections and Rehabilitation. (2008). *Historical Trends, 1987-2007.* Sacramento, CA: Offender Information Services Branch.

Caulkins, J. P. (2001). How large should the strike zone be in "Three Strikes and You're Out" sentencing laws? *Journal of Quantitative Criminology, 17*(3), 227-246.

Chen, E. Y. (2008). Impacts of "Three Strikes and You're Out" on crime trends in California and throughout the United States. *Journal of Contemporary Criminal Justice, 24*(4), 345-370.

Dickey, W. J. & Hollenhorst, P. (1999). Three-strikes laws: Five years later. *Corrections Management Quarterly, 3*(3), 1-18.

Eskridge, C. W. (2004). *Criminal justice: Concepts and issues* (4th ed.). Los Angeles, CA: Roxbury Publishing.

Gatland, L. (1998). Three strikes a soft pitch. *ABA Journal, 84,* 29.

Gottschalk, M. (2006). Dismantling the carceral state: The future of penal policy reform. *Texas Law Review, 84*(7), 1693-1749.

Irwin, J., Schiraldi, V., & Ziedenberg, J. (2000). America's one million nonviolent prisoners. *Social Justice, 27*(2), 135-147.

Jennings, W. G. (2006). Revisiting prediction models in policing: Identifying high-risk offenders. *American Journal of Criminal Justice, 31*(1), 35-50.

Johnson, J. L. & Saint-Germain, M. A. (2005). Officer down: Implications of three strikes for public safety. *Criminal Justice Policy Review, 16*(4), 443-460.

Justice Policy Institute. (2004). *Three strikes and you're out: An examination of the impact of 3-strikes laws 10 years after their enactment.* Washington, DC: Author.

Kelly, J. & Datta, A. (2009). Does three strikes really deter? A statistical analysis of its impact on crime rates in California. *College Teaching Methods & Styles, 5*(1), 29-36.

Kovandzic V, T. Sloan III, J. J., & Vieraitis, L. M. (2004). "Striking out" as crime reduction policy: The impact of "Three Strikes" laws on crime rates in U.S. cities. *Justice Quarterly, 21*(2), 207-239.

LaCourse, D. (1994). Three strikes is working in Washington. *Journal of Interpersonal Violence, 9*(3), 421-424.

Meehan, K. E. (2000). California's three-strikes law: The first six years. *Corrections Management Quarterly, 4*(4), 22-33.

Peak, K. J. (2010). *Justice administration: Police, courts, and corrections management* (6th ed.). Upper Saddle River, NJ: Pearson Education.

Pfaff, J. F. (2008). The empirics of prison growth: A critical review and path forward. *Journal of Criminal Law & Criminology, 98*(2), 547-619.

Stolzenberg, L. & D'Alessio, S. J. (1997). "Three Strikes and You're Out": The impact of California's new mandatory sentencing law on serious crime rates. *Crime & Delinquency, 43*(4), 457-469.

Washington State Department of Corrections. (2012). *Major sentencing changes impacting community supervision caseloads and prison population*. Olympia: Washington Statistical Analysis Center.

Willis, J. J. (2007). Punishment and democracy: Three strikes and you're out in California. *Crime, Law and Social Change, 47*(2), 121-123.

Chapter III:

Bhati, A. S. & Piquero, A. R. (2007). Estimating the impact of incarceration on subsequent offending trajectories: Deterrent, criminogenic, or null effect? *Journal of Criminal Law & Criminology, 98*(1), 207-253.

Bottcher, J. & Ezell, M. E. (2005). Examining the effectiveness of boot camps: A randomized experiment with a long-term follow up. *Journal of Research in Crime and Delinquency, 42*(3), 309-332.

Bridges, A. (1998). Increasing offender employability. *Probation Journal, 45*(2), 10.

Chen, E. Y. (2008). Impacts of "three strikes and you're out" on crime trends in California and throughout the United States. *Journal of Contemporary Criminal Justice, 24*(4), 345-370.

Colins, O., Vermeiren, R., Vahl, P., Markus, M., Broekaert, E., & Doreleijiers, T. (2011). Psychiatric disorder in detained male adolescents as risk factor for serious recidivism. *Canadian Journal of Psychiatry, 56*(1), 44-50.

Davidson, W. S., Jimenez, T. R., Onifade, E., & Hankins, S. S. (2010). Student experiences of the Adolescent Diversion Project: A community-based exemplar in the pedagogy of service-learning. *American Journal of Community Psychology, 46*(3), 442-458.

Davidson, W. S., Redner, R., Blakely, C. H., Mitchell, C. M., & Emshoff, J. G. (1987). Diversion of juvenile offenders: An experimental comparison. *Journal of Consulting and Clinical Psychology, 55*(1), 68-75.

Douglas, K. S., Epstein, M. E., & Poythress, N. G. (2008). Criminal recidivism among juvenile offenders: Testing the incremental and predictive validity of three measures of psychopathic features. *Law and Human Behavior, 32*(5), 423-438.

Duwe, G. & Kerschner, D. (2008). Removing a nail from the boot camp coffin: An outcome evaluation of Minnesota's Challenge Incarceration Program. *Crime & Delinquency, 54*(4), 614-643.

Eskridge, C. W. (2004). *Criminal justice: Concepts and issues* (4th ed.). Los Angeles, CA: Roxbury Publishing.

Gottschalk, M. (2006). Dismantling the carceral state: The future of penal policy reform. *Texas Law Review, 84*, 1693-1749.

Graffam, J., Shinkfield, A. J., & Hardcastle, L. (2008). The perceived employability of ex-prisoners and offenders. *International Journal of Offender Therapy and Comparative Criminology, 52*(6), 673-685.

Hancock, P. G. & Raeside, R. (2009). Modeling factors central to recidivism: An investigation of sentence management in the Scottish Prison Service. *The Prison Journal, 89*(1), 99-118.

Harris, A. (2007). Diverting and abdicating judicial discretion: Cultural, political, and procedural dynamics in California juvenile justice. *Law & Society Review, 41*(2), 387-427.

Jones, M. & Ross, D. L. (1997). Electronic house arrest and boot camp in North Carolina: Comparing recidivism. *Criminal Justice Policy Review, 8*(4), 383-403.

Kempinen, C. A. & Kurlychek, M. C. (2003). An outcome evaluation of Pennsylvania's boot camp: Does rehabilitative programming within a disciplinary setting reduce recidivism?. *Crime & Delinquency, 49*(4), 581-602.

Kilgore, D. & Meade, S. (2004). "Look what boot camp's done for me": Teaching and learning at Lakeview Academy. *Journal of Correctional Education, 55*(2), 170-185.

Kubrin, C. E. & Stewart, E. A. (2006). Predicting who reoffends: The neglected role of neighborhood context in recidivism studies. *Criminology, 44*(1), 165-197.

Kunselman, J. C. & Vito, G. F. (2002). Questioning mandatory sentencing efficiency: A case study of persistent felony offender rapists in Kentucky. *American Journal of Criminal Justice, 27*(1), 53-68.

Leschied, A. W., Austin, G. W., & Jaffe, P. G. (1988). Impact of the Young Offenders Act on recidivism rates of special needs youth: Clinical and policy implications. *Canadian Journal of Behavioural Science, 20*(3), 322-331.

Lussier, P. & Davies, G. (2011). A person-oriented perspective on sexual offenders, offending trajectories, and risk of recidivism: A new challenge for policymakers, risk assessors, and actuarial prediction? *Psychology, Public Policy, and Law, 17*(4), 530-561.

MacKenzie, D. L., Brame, R., McDowall, D., & Souryal, C. (1995). Boot camp prisons and recidivism in eight states. *Criminology, 33*(3), 327-357.

Nally, J., Lockwood, S., Knutson, K., & Ho, T. (2012). An evaluation of the effect of correctional education programs on post-release recidivism and employment: An empirical study in Indiana. *Journal of Correctional Education, 63*(1), 69-88.

Reid-MacNevin, S.A. (1997). Boot camps for young offenders: A politically acceptable punishment. *Journal of Contemporary Criminal Justice, 13*(2), 155-171.

Stincomb, J. B. (1999). Recovering from the shocking reality of shock incarceration. *Corrections Management Quarterly, 3*(4), 43-52.

Varghese, F. P., Hardin, E. E., Bauer, R. L., & Morgan, R. D. (2010). Attitudes toward hiring offenders: The roles of criminal history, job qualifications, and race. *International Journal of Offender Therapy and Comparative Criminology, 54*(5), 769-782.

Vennard, J. & Hedderman, C. (2009). Helping offenders into employment: How far is voluntary sector expertise valued in a contracting-out environment? *Criminology and Criminal Justice, 9*(2), 225-245.

Chapter IV:

Berry, R. M. (2005). Informed consent law, ethics, and practice: From infancy to reflective adolescence. *HEC Forum, 17*(1), 64-81.

Bhutta, Z. A. (2004). Beyond informed consent. World Health Organization. *Bulletin of the World Health Organization, 82*(10), 771-777.

Bloomberg, S. A. & Wilkins, L. T. (1977). Ethics of research involving human subjects in criminal justice. *Crime & Delinquency, 23*(4), 435-444.

Bond, T. (1992). Confidentiality: Counseling, ethics and the law. *Journal of Workplace Learning, 4*(4), 4-9.

Doblin, R. (1998). Dr. Leary's Concord Prison Experiment: A 34-year follow-up study. *Journal of Psychoactive Drugs, 30*(4), 419-426.

Erlen, J. A. (2010). Informed consent: Revisiting the issues. *Orthopaedic Nursing, 29*(4), 276-80.

Juritzen, T. I., Grimen, H., & Heggen, K. (2011). Protecting vulnerable research participants: A Foucault-inspired analysis of ethics committees. *Nursing Ethics, 18*(5), 640-650.

Kauzlarich, D. & Kramer, R. C. (1998). *Crimes of the American nuclear state: At home and abroad*. Boston, MA: Northern University Press.

Lowman, J. & Palys, T. (2001). The ethics and law of confidentiality in criminal justice research: A comparison of Canada and the United States. *International Criminal Justice Review, 11*(1), 1-33.

Mulvey, E. P. & Phelps, P. (1988). Ethical balances in juvenile justice research and practice. *American Psychologist, 43*(1), 65-69.

O'Neill, O. (2003). Some limits of informed consent. *Journal of Medical Ethics, 29*(1), 4.

Reeder, G. D., Monroe, A. E., & Pryor, J. B. (2008). Impressions of Milgram's obedient teachers: Situational cues inform inferences about motives and traits. *Journal of Personality and Social Psychology, 95*(1), 1-17.

Reverby, S. M. (2011). "Normal exposure" and inoculation syphilis: A PHS "Tuskegee" doctor in Guatemala, 1946-1948. *Journal of Policy History, 23*(1), 6-28.

Rhineberger, G. M. (2006). Research methods and research ethics coverage in criminal justice and criminology textbooks. *Journal of Criminal Justice Education, 17*(2), 279-296, 398.

Richardson, L. S. (2009). When human experimentation is criminal. *Journal of Criminal Law & Criminology, 99*(1), 89-133.

Semeniuk, I. (2010). A shocking discovery. *Nature, 467*(7316), 645.

Waltz, E. (2006). US ponders unlocking the gates to prisoner research. *Nature Medicine, 12*(1), 3.

Webb, P. (2008). Privacy or publicity: Media coverage and juvenile justice proceedings in the United States. *International Journal of Criminal Justice Sciences, 3*(1), 1-14.

Chapter V:

American Civil Liberties Union (ACLU). (October 6, 2005). Unregulated Use of Taser Stun Guns Threatens Lives, ACLU of Northern California Finds [Article]. Retrieved from http://www.aclu.org /racial-justice_prisoners-rights_drug-law-reform _immigrants-rights/unregulated-use-taser-stun-guns-th

Ferrell, Benjamin B. (May, 1988). Duty to Intervene: An Officer's Dilemma. *Journal of Contemporary Criminal Justice.* 4(2) 93-105.

Griffin, Sean P. & Bernard, Thomas J. (March, 2003). Angry Aggression Among Police Officers. *Police Quarterly.* 6(1) 3-21.

Miller, Michael E. (September, 2010). Taser Use and the Use-of-Force Continuum: Examining the Effect of Policy Change. *The Police Chief.* 77(9) 72–76.

Son, In Soo & Rome, Dennis M. (June, 2004). The Prevalence and Visibility of Police Misconduct: A Survey of Citizens and Police Officers. *Police Quarterly.* 7(2) 179-204.

U.S. Department of Justice: Office of Justice Programs. Adams, Kenneth, Alpert, Geoffrey P., Dunham, Roger G., Garner, Joel H., Greenfeld, Lawrence A., Henriquez, Mark A., et al. (October, 1999). *Use of Force by Police: Overview of National and Local Data.* Retrieved from http://www.ncjrs.gov/pdffiles1/nij/176330-1.pdf

Chapter VI:

Gottschalk, P. (2011). Management challenges in law enforcement: The case of police misconduct and crime. *International Journal of Law and Management, 53*(3), 169-181.

Lamboo, T. (2010). Police misconduct: Accountability of internal investigations. *The International Journal of Public Sector Management, 23*(7), 613-631.

Miller, S. (2010). Integrity systems and professional reporting in police organizations. *Criminal Justice Ethics, 29*(3), 241-257.

Rothwell, G. R. & Baldwin, J. N. (2007). Whistle-blowing and the code of silence in police agencies: Policy and structural predictors. *Crime & Delinquency, 53*(4), 605-632.

Shockey-Eckles, M. L. (2011). Police culture and the perpetuation of the officer shuffle: The paradox of life behind "the blue wall". *Humanity & Society, 35*(3), 290-309.

Wolfe, S. E. & Piquero, A. R. (2011). Organizational justice and police misconduct. *Criminal Justice and Behavior, 38*(4), 332-353.

Chapter VII:

Davis, J. A. & Lauber, K. M. (1999, August). Criminal behavioral assessment of arsonists, pyromaniacs, and multiple firesetters: The burning question. *Journal of Contemporary Criminal Justice, 15*(3), 273-290.

Dougals, J. & Olshaker, M. (1999). *The anatomy of motive*. New York, NY: Simon & Schuster, Inc.

Kocsis, R. N., & Cooksey, R. W. (2002, December). Criminal psychological profiling of serial   arson crimes. *International Journal of Offender Therapy and Comparative Criminology, 46*(6), 631-656.

United States Fire Administration. (2001, December). *Arson in the United States* (Topical Fire Research Series, *1*(8). Washington, DC: US Government Printing Office. Retrieved August 28, 2011, from http://www.usfa.dhs.gov /downloads/pdf/tfrs/v1i8-508.pdf

Chapter VIII:

Einat, T. & Einat, A. (August, 2008). Learning Disabilities and Delinquency: A Study of Israeli Prison Inmates. *International Journal of Offender Therapy and Comparative Criminology*. 52(4) 416-434.

Kafka, M. P. & Hennen, J. (October, 2002). A DSM-IV Axis I Comorbidity Study of Males (n=120) With Paraphilias and Paraphilia-Related Disorders. *Sexual Abuse: A Journal of Research and Treatment*. 14(4) 349-366.

Miller, K. P. (Director). (2008). *Generation Rx*. [Motion picture]. United States. Common Radius Films.

Mulsow, M. H., O'Neal, K. K., & McBride-Murry, V. (January, 2001). Adult Attention Deficit Hyperactivity Disorder, the Family, and Child Maltreatment. *Trauma, Violence, & Abuse*. 2(1) 36-50.

Robins, L. & Rutter, M. (1990). *Straight and Devious Pathways from Childhood to Adulthood*. New York: Cambridge University Press.

Savolainen, J., Hurtig, T. M., Ebeling, H. E., Moilanen, I. K., Hughes, L. A., & Taanila, A. M. (October 21, 2010). Attention deficit hyperactivity   disorder (ADHD) and criminal behaviour: the role of adolescent marginalization. *European Journal of Criminology*. 7(6) 442-459.

Vitelli, R. (December, 1996). Prevalence of Child Conduct and Attention-Deficit Hyperactivity Disorders in Adult Maximum Security-Inmates. *International Journal of Offender Therapy and Comparative Criminology*. 40(4) 263-271.

Westmoreland, P., Gunter, T., Loveless, P., Allen, J., Sieleni, B., & Black, D. W. (June, 2010). Attention Deficit Hyperactivity Disorder in Men and Women Newly Committed to Prison: Clinical Characteristics, Psychiatric Comorbidity, and Quality of Life. *International Journal of Offender Therapy and Comparative Criminology*. 54(3) 361-377.

Chapter IX:

Monin, B., Sawyer, P. J. & Marquez, M. J. (2008, July). The rejection of moral rebels: Resenting those who do the right thing. *Journal of Personality and Social Psychology, 95(1)*, 76-93.

Reeder, G. D., Monroe, A. E. & Pryor, J. B. (2008, July). Impressions of Milgram's obedient teachers: Situational cues inform inferences about motives and traits. *Journal of Personality and Social Psychology, 95(1)*, 1-17.

Smith, E. & Mackie, D. (2007). *Social psychology (3rd ed).* Psychology Press.

Chapter X:

American Psychiatric Association. (2000). *Diagnostic and statistical manual of mental disorders* (Revised 4th ed.). Washington, DC: Author.

BBC. (2006, August 16). *Shot at dawn, pardoned 90 years on.* Retrieved from http://news.bbc.co.uk/2/hi/uk_news /england/4798025.stm

Bell, D. (1956). The theory of mass society. *Commentary, 22(1),* 75-83.

Bentley, S. (2005). *A short history of PTSD: From Thermopylae to Hue soldiers have always had a disturbing reaction to war.* Retrieved from http://www.vva.org/archive/ TheVeteran/2005_03/feature_HistoryPTSD.htm

Catherall, D. R. (1986). The support system and amelioration of PTSD in Vietnam veterans. *Psychotherapy: Theory, Research, Practice, Training, 23(3),* 472-482.

Charvat, M. (2010). *History of Post-traumatic Stress Disorder in combat* [PowerPoint slides]. Retrieved from http://www.warrelatedillness.va.gov/WARRELATEDILLNESS /education/conferences/2010-sept/slides/2010_09_14_ CharvatM-History-of-PTSD-in-Combat.ppt

Davids, T. W. R. (1880). *Buddhist birth stories; or Jataka tales. The oldest collection of folk-lore extant: Being the Jatakatthavannana.* Boston, MA: Houghton, Miffin, & Co.

Department of Veterans Affairs. (2004). *VA fact sheet: World War II veterans by the numbers.* Washington, DC: Author.

Dickens, C. (1880 / 2008). *The letters of Charles Dickens – Vol. 2, 1857-1870*. London, UK: Chapman & Hall.

Foucalt, M. (1965). *Madness and civilization: A history of insanity in the age of reason*. (R. Howard, Trans.). New York, NY: Random House. (Original work published 1961).

Fussell, P. (1989). *Wartime: Understanding and behavior in the Second World War*. New York, NY: Oxford University Press.

Gabriel, R. A. (1987). *No more heroes: Madness and psychiatry in war*. New York, NY: Macmillan.

Gandolfini, J. (Producer), Alpert, J., Goosenberg-Kent, E., & O'Neill, M. (Directors). (2010). *Wartorn: 1861-2010* [Motion picture]. United States: Home Box Office.

Grossman, D. (2000). *On sheep, wolves and sheepdogs*. Retrieved from http://www.killology.com/sheep_dog.htm

Hamblen, J. (2009). *PTSD 101 Courses: What is PTSD?* [Adobe Flash presentation]. Retrieved from http://www.ptsd.va.gov/professional/ptsd101/course-modules/what-is-ptsd.asp

Harper, C. L. & Leicht, K. T. (2011). *Exploring social change: American and the world* (6th ed.). Upper Saddle River, NJ: Pearson Prentice Hall.

Haughn, C. & Gonsiorek, J. C. (2009). The Book of Job: Implications for construct validity of posttraumatic stress disorder diagnostic criteria. *Mental Health, Religion & Culture, 12*(8), 833-845.

Homer. (1998). *The iliad*. (R. Fagles, Trans.). New York, NY: Penguin Classics. (Original work published 730 BCE).

Jayatunge, R. M. (2012). *Post-Traumatic Stress Disorder (PTSD) – A malady shared by east and west* [PowerPoint slides]. Retrieved from http://fmso.leavenworth.army.mil/Collaboration/international/Sri%20Lanka/PTSD.pdf

Jung, C. G. (2010). *Answer to Job*. (R. F. C. Hull, Trans.). Princeton, NJ: Princeton University Press. (Original work published 1952).

Kaeuper, R. W., & Kennedy, E. (Eds.). (1996). *The book of chivalry of Geoffroi de Charny: Text, context, and translation*. Philadelphia, PA: University of Pennsylvania Press.

Mitchell, T. J. (2010). *History of the Great War based on official documents: Medical services, casualties and medical statistics.* Uckfield, UK: Naval and Military Press.

Mokros, A., Menner, B., Eisenbarth, H., Alpers, G. W., Lange, K. W., & Osterheider, M. (2008). Diminished cooperativeness of psychopaths in a prisoner's dilemma game yields higher rewards. *The Journal of Abnormal Psychology, 117*(2), 406-413.

Nixon, R. (1985). *No more Vietnams.* New York, NY: Arbor House.

Price, J. L. (2007). *Findings from the National Vietnam Veterans' Readjustment Study.* Retrieved from http://www.ptsd.va.gov/ professional/pages/vietnam-vets-study.asp

Rosen, G. (Ed.). (2004). *Posttraumatic Stress Disorder: Issues and controversies.* Indianapolis, IN: Wiley.

Sayer, N.A., Friedmann-Sanchez, G., Spoont, M., Murdock, M., Parker, L.E., Chiros, C., & Rosenheck, R. (2009). A qualitative study of determinants of PTSD treatment initiation in veterans. *Psychiatry, 72*(3), 238-255.

Shakespeare, W. (1597 / 2010). *King Henry IV, part 1.* Fairfield, IA: Akasha Publishing.

Shakespeare, W. (1603 / 1993). *Macbeth.* Mineola, NY: Dover Publications.

Trimble, M.D. (1985). Post-Traumatic Stress Disorder: History of a concept. In C.R. Figley (Ed.), *Trauma and its wake: The study and treatment of Post-Traumatic Stress Disorder.* New York, NY: Brunner/Mazel. Revised from Encyclopedia of Psychology, R. Corsini, Ed. (New York, NY: Wiley, 1984, 1994).

Van der Kolk, B. A., Brown, P., & Van der Hart, O. (1989). Pierre Janet on post-traumatic stress. *Journal of Traumatic Stress, 2*(4), 365-378.

Chapter XI:

Allen, W. D. (2007). The reporting and underreporting of rape. *Southern Economic Journal, 73*(3), 623-641.

Askin, K. D. (1999). Sexual violence in decisions and indictments of the Yugoslav and Rwandan tribunals: Current status. *The American Journal of International Law, 93*(1), 97-123.

Baaz, M. E. & Stern, M. (2009). Why do soldiers rape? Masculinity, violence, and sexuality in the armed forces in the Congo (DRC). *International Studies Quarterly, 53*(2), 495-518.

Barker, V. (2007). The politics of pain: A political Institutionalist analysis of crime victims' moral protests. *Law & Society Review, 41*(3), 619-663.

Bergoffen, D. B. (2006). From genocide to justice: Women's bodies as a legal writing pad. *Feminist Studies, 32*(1), 11-37, 192.

Bijleveld, C., Morssinkhof, A., & Smeulers, A. (2009). Counting the countless: Rape victimization during the Rwandan genocide. *International Criminal Justice Review, 19*(2), 208-224.

Bristol, N. (2006). Military incursions into aid work anger humanitarian groups. *The Lancet, 367*(9508), 384-386.

Buss, D. E. (2009). Rethinking 'rape as a weapon of war'. *Feminist Legal Studies, 17*(2), 145-163.

Castillo, P. (2007). Rethinking deterrence: The International Criminal Court in Sudan. *UNISCI Discussion Papers, 13*, 167-184.

Clay-Warner, J. & McMahon-Howard, J. (2009). Rape reporting: "Classic rape" and the behavior of law. *Violence and Victims, 24*(6), 723-743.

Clifford, C. (2008). *Rape as a weapon of war and its long-term effects on victims and society.* Paper presented at the 7th Global Conference: Violence and the Contexts of Hostility. Budapest, Hungary.

Donovan, P. (2002). Rape and HIV/AIDS in Rwanda. *The Lancet, 360*, s17-18.

Durkham, H. & O'Byrne, K. (2010). The dialogue of difference: Gender perspectives on international humanitarian law. *International Review of the Red Cross, 92*(877), 31-52.

Dwyer, P. G. (2009). "It still makes me shudder": Memories of massacres and atrocities during the Revolutionary and Napoleonic Wars. *War in History, 16*(4), 381-405.

Epp, M. (1997). The memory of violence: Soviet and East European Mennonite refugees and rape in the Second World War. *Journal of Women's History, 9*(1), 58-87.

Falcon, S. (2001). Rape as a weapon of war: Advancing human rights for women at the U.S.-Mexico border. *Social Justice, 28*(2), 31-50.

Feldberg, G. (1997). Defining the facts of rape: The use of medical evidence in sexual assault trials. *Canadian Journal of Women & the Law, 9*(1), 89-114.

Ferraro, K. J. (2008). Taken by force: Rap and American GIs in Europe during WWII. *Contemporary Sociology, 37*(6), 585-586.

Ghobarah, H. A., Huth, P., & Russett, B. (2003). Civil wars kill and maim people - Long after the shooting stops. *The American Political Science Review, 97*(2), 189-202.

Gottschall, J. (2004). Explaining wartime rape. *The Journal of Sex Research, 41*(2), 129-136.

Haddad, H. N. (2011). Mobilizing the will to prosecute: Crimes of rape at the Yugoslav and Rwandan Tribunals. *Human Rights Review, 12*(1), 109-132.

Hagan, J., Rymond-Richmond, W., & Parker, P. (2005). The criminology of genocide: The death and rape of Darfur. *Criminology, 43*(3), 525-561.

Halley, J. (2008). Rape in Berlin: Reconsidering the criminalization of rape in the international law of armed conflict. *Melbourne Journal of International Law, 9*(1), 78-124.

Hargreaves, S. (2001). Rape as a war crime: Putting policy into practice. *The Lancet, 357*(9258), 737.

Hastings, J. A. (2002). Silencing state-sponsored rape: In and beyond a transnational Guatemalan community. *Violence Against Women, 8*(10), 1153-1181.

Hoffman, M. H. (1999). Is the Holocaust unique?: Perspectives on comparative genocide/the myth of rescue: Why the democracies could not have saved more Jews from the Nazis. *Parameters, 29*(1), 177-78.

Hogg, N. (2010). Women's participation in the Rwandan genocide: Mothers or monsters? *International Review of the Red Cross, 92*(877), 69-102.

Holmes, S. T. & Holmes, R. M. (2009). *Sex crimes: Patterns and behavior* (3rd ed.). Thousand Oaks, CA: SAGE.

Jamieson, R. (1999). Genocide and the social production of immorality. *Theoretical Criminology, 3*(2), 131-146.

Johnson, D. Peterson, J., Sommers, I., & Baskin, D. (2012). Use of forensic science in investigating crimes of sexual violence: Contrasting its theoretical potential with empirical realities. *Violence Against Women, 18*(2), 193-222.

Kauzlarich, D. & Kramer, R. C. (1998). *Crimes of the American nuclear state: At home and abroad.* Boston, MA: Northeastern University Press.

Koss, M. P. (1993). Rape: Scope, impact, interventions, and public policy responses. *American Psychologist, 48*(10), 1062-1069.

Leitenberg, M. (1994). Rwanda, 1994: International Incompetence produces genocide. *Peacekeeping & International Relations, 23*(6), 6-10.

MacDonald, D. B. (2005). Forgetting and denying: Iris Chang, the Holocaust and the challenge of Nanking. *International Politics, 42*(4), 403-427.

Maedl, A. (2011). Rape as a weapon of war in the Eastern DRC? The victims' perspective. *Human Rights Quarterly, 33*(1), 128-147, 261.

Malone, D. M. (2008). International criminal justice: Just an expensive mirage? *International Journal, 63*(3), 729-741.

Meini, B. (2008). HIV/AIDS, crime and security in Southern Africa. *African Journal of Criminology and Justice Studies: AJCJS, 3*(2), 35-84.

Mukamana, D. & Brysiewicz, P. (2008). The lived experience of genocide rape survivors in Rwanda. *Journal of Nursing Scholarship, 40*(4), 379-384.

Parfitt, T. (2004). Russian soldiers blamed for civilian rape in Chechnya. *The Lancet, 363*(9417), 1291.

Ross, A. (2004). Truth and consequences in Guatemala. *GeoJournal, 60*(1), 73-79.

Sedgwick, J. (2009). Memory on trial: Constructing and contesting the 'Rape of Nanking' at the International military tribunal for the Far East, 1946-1948. *Modern Asian Studies, 43*(5), 1229-1254.

Shanks, L. & Schull, M. J. (2000). Rape in war: The humanitarian response. *Canadian Medical Association Journal, 163*(9), 1152-1156.

Spohn, C. C. & Horney, J. (1996). The impact of rape law reform on the processing of simple and aggravated rape cases. *Journal of Criminal Law & Criminology, 86*(3), 861-884.

Staub, E. (1999). The origins and prevention of genocide, mass killing, and other collective violence. *Peace and Conflict: Journal of Peace Psychology, 5*(4), 303-336.

Thornberry, C. (1996). Saving the war crimes tribunal. *Foreign Policy, 104*, 72-86.

Thornhill, R. & Palmer, C. T. (2000). Why men rape. *Sciences, 40*(1), 30-36.

Valenius, J. (2004). *Living in an over-organized jungle: Military discipline, masculinity and rape in Casualties of War*. Paper presented at the Annual Meeting of the International Studies Association. Montreal, Canada.

Vandermassen, G. (2011). Evolution and rape: A feminist Darwinian perspective. *Sex Roles, 64*, 732-747.

Vikman, E. (2005). Ancient origins: Sexual violence in warfare, part I. *Anthropology & Medicine, 12*(1), 21-31.

Weiss, K. G. (2010). Too ashamed to report: Deconstructing the shame of sexual victimization. *Feminist Criminology, 5*(3), 286-310.

Weitsman, P. A. (2008). The politics of identity and sexual violence: A review of Bosnia and Rwanda. *Human Rights Quarterly, 30*(3), 561-578.

Whitmer, B. (2006). "Torture chambers and rape rooms": What Abu Ghraib can tell us about the American carceral system. *CR: The New Centennial Review, 6*(1), 171-194, 285.

Winnick, T. A. (2008). Another layer of ignominy: Beliefs about public views of sex offenders. *Sociological Focus, 41*(1), 53-70.

Zimbardo, P. (2007). *The Lucifer effect: Understanding how good people turn evil*. New York, NY: Random House.

Chapter XII:

Illustrations

Figure 1. 2004-07: Smith, J. (Producer). (2010, October 4). *The Rachel Maddow show* [Television broadcast]. New York, NY: National Broadcasting Company.

2008-11: New America Foundation. (2012). The year of the drone: An analysis of U.S. drone strikes in Pakistan, 2004-2012. Retrieved from http://counterterrorism.newamerica.net/drones

Figure 2. New America Foundation. (2012). The year of the drone: An analysis of U.S. drone strikes in Pakistan, 2004-2012. Retrieved from http://counterterrorism.newamerica.net/drones

Sources

Anderson, B. (2010). Morale and the affective geographies of the 'war on terror'. *Cultural Geographies, 17*(2), 219-236.

Arreguin-Toft, I. (2006). *How the weak win wars: A theory of asymmetric conflict.* New York, NY: Cambridge University Press.

Everett, W. J. (1997). Max Weber and democratic politics. *Theological Studies, 58*(2), 377-378.

Gailey, C. W. (2003). Community, state and questions of social evolution in Marx's ethnological notebooks. *Anthropologica, 45*(1), 45-57.

Gladwell, M. (Presenter). (2011, October 26). Malcolm Gladwell: The strange tale of the Norden bombsight. *TED Talks.* Podcast retrieved from http://www.youtube.com/watch?v=HpiZTvlWx2g

Khan, Z. (2012, August 31) US drone strike kills five militants in Pakistan. *Associated Press.* Retrieved from http://abcnews.go.com/International/wireStory/pakistan-killed-car-bombing-northwest-17126058

Meilinger, P. S. (1996). Trenchard and "morale bombing": The evolution of Royal Air Force doctrine before World War II. *The Journal of Military History, 60*(2), 243-270.

New America Foundation. (2012). The year of the drone: An analysis of U.S. drone strikes in Pakistan, 2004-2012. Retrieved fromhttp://counterterrorism.newamerica. net/drones

Obama, B. (2012, June 15). Presidential letter – 2012 War Powers Resolution 6-month report. Retrieved from http://www.whitehouse.gov/the-press-office/2012/ 06/15/presidential-letter-2012-war-powers-resolution-6-month-report

Ritzer, G. (2011). *Classical sociological theory* (6th ed.). New York, NY: McGraw-Hill.

Semple, M. (2012). Afghanistan and Pakistan: Conflict, extremism, and resistance to modernity. *The Middle East Journal, 66*(2), 374-375.

Smith, J. (Producer). (2012, June 30). *The Rachel Maddow show* [Television broadcast]. New York, NY: National Broadcasting Company.

Smith, J. (Producer). (2010, October 4). *The Rachel Maddow show* [Television broadcast]. New York, NY: National Broadcasting Company.

Swedberg, R. (2003). The changing picture of Max Weber's sociology. *Annual Review of Sociology, 29*, 283-306.

Weber, M. (1991). *From Max Weber: Essays in sociology.* H.H. Gerth & C.W. Mills (Eds.). New York, NY: Routledge Classics.

Wong, Y. (2000). Max Weber, democracy and modernization. *Contemporary Sociology, 29*(3), 560-562.

Chapter XIII:

Brands, H.W. (2009). Hesitant emancipator. *American History, 44*(2), 54-59.

Cook, R. (2001). Abraham Lincoln: Redeemer President. *The Journal of American History, 88*(2), 650-651.

Dirck, B. (2009). Father Abraham: Lincoln's relentless struggle to end slavery/ Act of justice: Lincoln's Emancipation Proclamation and the law of war/ Lincoln and freedom: Slavery, emancipation, and the Thirteenth Amendment. *Civil War History, 55*(3), 382-385.

Foner, E. (2011). The Civil War in 'postracial' America. *Nation, 293*(15), 24-26.

Gienapp, W. (2002). *Abraham Lincoln and Civil War America: A biography.* New York, NY: Oxford University Press.

Gilmore, M. (2006). A plot against America: Free speech and the American Renaissance. *Raritan, 26*(2), 90-113.

Guelzo, A. (2002). Defending emancipation: Abraham Lincoln and the Conkling Letter, 1863. *Civil War History, 48*(4), 313-337.

Manning, C. (2012). All for the Union…and emancipation, too what the Civil War was about. *Dissent, 59*(1), 91-95.

McColley, R. (2005). Special review essay: Recent books on Abraham Lincoln. *Journal of the Illinois State Historical Society, 98*(4), 303-311.

Wilson, K. (2008). Lincoln and freedom: Slavery, emancipation, and the Thirteenth Amendment. *The Journal of American History, 95*(2), 544-545.

Zinn, H. (2003). *A people's history of the United States: Abridged teaching edition.* New York, NY: The New Press.

Chapter XIV:

Illustrations

All figures and tables in this chapter were taken from the author's original research.

Sources

Brumbaugh, S. M., Sanchez, L. A., Nock, S. L., & Wright, J. D. (2008). Attitudes toward gay marriage in states undergoing marriage law transformation. *Journal of Marriage and Family, 70*(2), 345-359.

Newport, F. (2012). Religion big factor for Americans against Same-Sex Marriage. Retrieved from http://www.gallup.com/poll/159089/religion-major-factor-americans-opposed-sex-marriage.aspx

Siegle, D. (2012). Critical values of the Pearson product-moment correlation coefficient. Retrieved from http://www.gifted.uconn.edu/siegle/research/correlation/corrchrt.htm

Smith, C., Faris, R., Denton, M. L., Regnerus, M. (2003). Mapping American adolescent subjective religiosity and attitudes of alienation toward religion: A research report. *Sociology of Religion, 64*(1), 111-133.

Wilkinson, W. W. & Roys, A. C. (2005). The components of sexual orientation, religiosity, and heterosexuals' impressions of gay men and lesbians. *The Journal of Social Psychology, 145*(1), 65-83.

Chapter XV:

Ashworth, R. A. (1920). The survival of Christianity. *The Biblical Word, 54*(3), 282-287.

Brudney, D. (2005). On noncoercive establishment. *Political Theory, 33*(6), 812-839.

Cole, S. (2004). Merton's contribution to the sociology of science. *Social Studies of Science, 34*(6), 829-844.

Demerath III, N. J. (1996). Who now debates functionalism? From "system, change and conflict" to "culture, choice, and praxis". *Sociological Forum, 11*(2), 333-345.

Martin, D. (1979). Talcott Parsons: 1902-1979. *The British Journal of Sociology, 30*(3), 265-266.

Nelkin, D. (2004). God talk: Confusion between science and religion: Posthumous essay. *Science, Technology, & Human Values, 29*(2), 139-152.

Orr, H. A. (2009). Darwin and Darwinism: The (alleged) social implications of the origin of species. *Genetics, 183*(3), 767-772.

Powell, L. H. & Jorgensen, S. R. (1985). Evaluation of a church-based sexuality education program for adolescents. *Family Relations, 34*(4), 475-482.

Ritzer, G. (2011). *Classical sociological theory* (6th ed.). New York, NY: McGraw-Hill.

Ryan, P. J. (2005). A case study in the cultural origins of a superpower: Liberal individualism, American nationalism, and the rise of high school life, a study of Cleveland's Central and East technical high schools, 1890-1918. *History of Education Quarterly, 45*(1), 66-95.

Turner, B. S. (1993). Talcott Parsons, universalism and the educational revolution: Democracy versus professionalism. *The British Journal of Sociology, 44*(1), 1-24.

Chapter XVI:

Ajdacic-Gross, V. Killias, M., Hepp, U., Gadola, E., Bopp, M., Lauber, C., Schnyder, U., Gutzwiller, F., & Rossler, W. (2006). Changing times: A longitudinal analysis of international firearm suicide data. *American Journal of Public Health, 96*(10), 1752-5.

Ajdacic-Gross, V., Weiss, M. G., Ring, M., Hepp, U., Bopp, M., Gutzwiller, F., & Rossler, W. (2008). Methods of suicide: International suicide patterns derived from the WHO mortality database. *Bulletin of the World Health Organization, 86*(9), 726-32.

Altheimer, I. (2010). An exploratory analysis of guns and violent crime in a cross-national sample of cities. *The Southwest Journal of Criminal Justice, 6*(3), 204-27.

Brent, D. A. & Bridge, J. (2003). Firearm availability and suicide: Evidence, interventions, and future directions. *The American Behavioral Scientist, 46*(9), 1192-1210.

Birckmayer, J. & Hemenway, D. (2001). Suicide and firearm prevalence: Are youth disproportionately affected? *Suicide and Life-Threatening Behavior, 31*(3), 303-310.

Centers for Disease Control and Prevention. (2011). *National vital statistics reports: Deaths, final data for 2009* (DHHS Publication No. PHS-2012-1120). Washington, DC: U.S. Government Printing Office.

Chapman, S., Alpers, P. Agho, K., & Jones, M. (2006). Australia's 1996 gun law reforms: Faster falls in firearm deaths, firearm suicides, and a decade without mass shootings. *Injury Prevention, 12*(6), 365-72.

Federal Bureau of Investigation. (2011). *Expanded homicide data table 15: Justifiable homicide by weapon, private citizen, 2006-2010* [Data file]. Retrieved from http://www.fbi.gov/about-us/cjis/ucr/crime-in-the-u.s/2010/crime-in-the-u.s.-2010/tables/10shrtbl15.xls

Graduate Institute of International and Development Studies. (2011). *Small arms survey 2012: Moving targets.* Cambridge, UK: Author.

Hepburn, L. M. & Hemenway, D. (2004). Firearm availability and homicide: A review of the literature. *Aggression and Violent Behavior, 9*(4), 417-40.

Hoskin, A. W. (2001). Armed Americans: The impact of firearm availability on national homicide rates. *Justice Quarterly, 18*(3), 569-92.

Kleck, G. (2004). Measures of gun ownership levels for macro-level crime and violence research. *Journal of Research in Crime and Delinquency, 41*(3), 3-36.

Kleck, G. (1997). *Targeting guns: Firearms and their control.* New York, NY: Walter de Gruyter, Inc.

Lemaire, J. (2005). The cost of firearm deaths in the United States: Reduced life expectancies and increased insurance costs. *Journal of Risk and Insurance, 72*(3), 359-74.

Library of Congress. (2012, August 8). United States: Gun ownership and the Supreme Court. Retrieved from http://www.loc.gov/law/help/second-amendment.php

Lott, J. R. J. (2000). *More guns less crime: Understanding crime and gun control laws* (2nd ed.). Chicago, IL: University of Chicago Press.

McDowall, D. (1991). Firearm availability and homicide rates in Detroit, 1951-1986. *Social Forces, 69*(4), 1085-1101.

Miller, M. Azrael, D., & Hemenway, D. (2002a). Firearm availability and unintentional firearm deaths, suicide, and homicide among 5-14 year olds. *The Journal of Trauma: Injury, Infection, and Critical Care, 52*(2), 267-74.

Miller, M., Azrael, D., & Hemenway, D. (2002b). Household firearm ownership and suicide rates in the United States. *Epidemiology, 13*(5), 517-24.

Miller, M., Azrael, D., & Hemenway, D. (2002c). Rates of household firearm ownership and homicide across US regions and states, 1988-1997. *American Journal of Public Health, 92*(12), 1988-93.

Miller, M., Azrael, D., Hepburn, L., Hemenway, D., & Lippmann, S. J. (2006). The association between changes in household firearm ownership and rates of suicide in the United States, 1981-2002. *Injury Prevention, 12*(3), 178-82.

Miller, M., Hemenway, D., Azrael, D. (2007). State-level homicide victimization rates in the US in relation to survey measures of household firearm ownership. *Social Science & Medicine, 64*(3), 656-64.

Miller, M., Lippmann, S. J., Azrael, D., & Hemenway, D. (2007). Household firearm ownership and rates of suicide across the 50 United States. *The Journal of Trauma, 62*(4), 1029-34.

Morgenstern, H. (1997). Gun availability and violent death. *American Journal of Public Health, 87*(6), 899-901.

Morrison, G. B. & Vila, B. J. (1998). Police handgun qualification: Practical measure or aimless activity? *Policing, 21*(3), 510-33.

Zimring, F. E. (1968). Is gun control likely to reduce violent killing? *University of Chicago Law Review, 35,* 721-37.

Zimring, F. E., & Hawkins, G. (1997). *Crime is not the problem: Lethal violence in America.* New York, NY: Oxford University Press.

www.ingramcontent.com/pod-product-compliance
Lightning Source LLC
Chambersburg PA
CBHW032000170526
45157CB00002B/485